WE HAVE TRIED . . .
to contain population explosion through birth control;
end the threat of nuclear holocaust by building bigger
missile systems; stave off world famine with new foods
and better ways of growing them; control disease
through improved sanitation and medicine; tackle the
problems of the ghettos through better housing and
transportation; design new ways of reducing or disposing of waste to stop the pollution of our environment.

Still, things grow worse.

If all of modern science and technology cannot significantly change man's environment, can mankind be
saved?

B. F. Skinner, the great behaviorist and the most influ-
ential and controversial psychologist of our time, suggests that what is called for now is a "technology of
behavior"—a systematic and scientific program to alter
the nature of Man.

A plan that would take Man
BEYOND FREEDOM AND DIGNITY . . .

weg: renew
p 25, 99, 115

B. F. SKINNER
Beyond Freedom
and
Dignity

A BANTAM/VINTAGE BOOK

BANTAM BOOKS
TORONTO/NEW YORK/LONDON

VINTAGE BOOKS
A Division of Random House
NEW YORK

To
JUSTINE
and
HER WORLD

*This low-priced Bantam Book
has been completely reset in a type face
designed for easy reading, and was printed
from new plates. It contains the complete
text of the original hard-cover edition.*
NOT ONE WORD HAS BEEN OMITTED.

BEYOND FREEDOM AND DIGNITY
*A Bantam/Vintage Book / published by arrangement with
Alfred A. Knopf, Inc.*

PRINTING HISTORY
*Knopf edition published September 1971
9 printings through March 1972*
Book-Of-The-Month Club edition published September 1971
PSYCHOLOGY TODAY *Magazine serialized August 1971*
NEW YORK POST *serialized in 12 parts March 1972*
*Bantam / Vintage edition / September 1972
15 printings through June 1980*

Back cover photo of the Author by Jill Krementz

ISBN 0-553-14372-7

Published simultaneously in the United States and Canada

*Bantam Books are published by Bantam Books, Inc. Its trade-
mark, consisting of the words "Bantam Books" and the portrayal of a bantam, is Registered in U.S. Patent and Trademark
Office and in other countries. Marca Registrada. Bantam
Books, Inc., 666 Fifth Avenue, New York, New York 10019.*

PRINTED IN THE UNITED STATES OF AMERICA

24 23 22 21 20 19 18 17 16

Contents

1
A Technology of Behavior

IN TRYING TO SOLVE the terrifying problems that face us in the world today, we naturally turn to the things we do best. We play from strength, and our strength is science and technology. To contain a population explosion we look for better methods of birth control. Threatened by a nuclear holocaust, we build bigger deterrent forces and anti-ballistic-missile systems. We try to stave off world famine with new foods and better ways of growing them. Improved sanitation and medicine will, we hope, control disease, better housing and transportation will solve the problems of the ghettos, and new ways of reducing or disposing of waste will stop the pollution of the environment. We can point to remarkable achievements in all these fields, and it is not surprising that we should try to extend them. But things grow steadily worse and it is disheartening to find that technology itself is increasingly at fault. Sanitation and medicine have made the problems of population more acute, war has acquired a new horror with the invention of nuclear weapons, and the affluent pursuit of happiness is largely responsible for pollution. As Darlington* has said, "Every new source from which man has increased his power on the earth has been used to diminish the prospects of his successors. All his progress has been made at the expense of damage to his environment which he cannot repair and could not foresee."

Whether or not he could have foreseen the damage, man must repair it or all is lost. And he can do so if he will recognize the nature of the difficulty. The application of the physical and biological sciences alone will not solve our problems because the solutions lie in another field. Better contraceptives will control population only if people use them. New weapons may offset new defenses and vice versa, but a nuclear holocaust can be prevented only if the conditions under which nations make war can be changed. New methods of agriculture and medicine will not help if they are not practiced, and housing is a matter not only of buildings and cities but of how people live. Overcrowding can be corrected only by inducing people not to crowd, and the environment will continue to deteriorate until polluting practices are abandoned.

In short, we need to make vast changes in human behavior, and we cannot make them with the help of nothing more than physics or biology, no matter how hard we try. (And there are other problems, such as the breakdown of our educational system and the disaffection and revolt of the young, to which physical and biological technologies are so obviously irrelevant that they have never been applied.) It is not enough to "use technology with a deeper understanding of human issues," or to "dedicate technology to man's spiritual needs," or to "encourage technologists to look at human problems." Such expressions imply that where human behavior begins, technology stops, and that we must carry on, as we have in the past, with what we have learned from personal experience or from those collections of personal experiences called history, or with the distillations of experience to be found in folk wisdom and practical rules of thumb. These have been available for centuries, and all we have to show for them is the state of the world today.

What we need is a technology of behavior. We could solve our problems quickly enough if we could adjust the growth of the world's population as precisely as we adjust the course of a spaceship, or improve agriculture and industry with some of the confidence with which we accelerate high-energy particles, or move toward a peaceful world with something like the steady progress with which physics has approached absolute zero (even though both remain presumably out of reach). But a behavioral technology comparable in power and precision to physical and biological technology is lacking, and those who do not find the very possibility ridiculous are more likely to be frightened by it than reassured. That is how far we are from "understanding human issues" in the sense in which physics and biology understand their fields, and how far we are from preventing the catastrophe toward which the world seems to be inexorably moving.

Twenty-five hundred years ago it might have been said that man understood himself as well as any other part of his world. Today he is the thing he understands least. Physics and biology have come a long way, but there has been no comparable development of anything like a science of human behavior. Greek physics and biology are now of historical interest only (no modern physicist or biologist would turn to Aristotle for help), but the dialogues of Plato are still assigned to students and cited as if they threw light on human behavior. Aristotle could not have understood a page of modern physics or biology, but Socrates and his friends would have little trouble in following most current discussions of human affairs. And as to technology, we have made immense strides in controlling the physical and biological worlds, but our practices in government, education, and much of economics, though adapted to very different conditions, have not greatly improved.

We can scarcely explain this by saying that the Greeks knew all there was to know about human behavior. Certainly they knew more than they knew about the physical world, but it was still not much. Moreover, their way of thinking about human behavior must have had some fatal flaw. Whereas Greek physics and biology, no matter how crude, led eventually to modern science, Greek theories of human behavior led nowhere. If they are with us today, it is not because they possessed some kind of eternal verity, but because they did not contain the seeds of anything better.

It can always be argued that human behavior is a particularly difficult field. It is, and we are especially likely to think so just because we are so inept in dealing with it. But modern physics and biology successfully treat subjects that are certainly no simpler than many aspects of human behavior. The difference is that the instruments and methods they use are of commensurate complexity. The fact that equally powerful instruments and methods are not available in the field of human behavior is not an explanation; it is only part of the puzzle. Was putting a man on the moon actually easier than improving education in our public schools? Or than constructing better kinds of living space for everyone? Or than making it possible for everyone to be gainfully employed and, as a result, to enjoy a higher standard of living? The choice was not a matter of priorities, for no one could have said that it was more important to get to the moon. The exciting thing about getting to the moon was its feasibility. Science and technology had reached the point at which, with one great push, the thing could be done. There is no comparable excitement about the problems posed by human behavior. We are not close to solutions.

It is easy to conclude that there must be something about human behavior which makes a scientific analysis, and hence an effective technology, impossible, but we have not by any means exhausted the possibilities. There is a sense in which it can be said that the methods of science have scarcely yet been applied to human behavior. We have used the instruments of science; we have counted and measured and compared; but something essential to scientific practice is missing in almost all current discussions of human behavior. It has to do with our treatment of the causes of behavior. (The term "cause" is no longer common in sophisticated scientific writing, but it will serve well enough here.)

Man's first experience with causes probably came from his own behavior: things moved because he moved them. If other things moved, it was because someone else was moving them, and if the mover could not be seen, it was because he was invisible. The Greek gods served in this way as the causes of physical phenomena. They were usually outside the things they moved, but they might enter into and "possess" them. Physics and biology soon abandoned explanations of this sort and turned to more useful kinds of causes, but the step has not been decisively taken in the field of human behavior. Intelligent people no longer believe that men are possessed by demons (although the exorcism of devils is occasionally practiced, and the daimonic has reappeared in the writings of psychotherapists), but human behavior is still commonly attributed to indwelling agents. A juvenile delinquent is said, for example, to be suffering from a disturbed personality. There would be no point in saying it if the personality were not somehow distinct from the body which has got itself into trouble. The distinction is clear when one body is said to contain several personalities which control it in different ways at different times. Psychoanalysts have identified three of these personalities—the ego, superego, and id—and interactions among them are said to be responsible for the behavior of the man in whom they dwell.

Although physics soon stopped personifying things in this way, it continued for a long time to speak as if they had wills, impulses, feelings, purposes, and other fragmentary attributes of an indwelling agent. According to Butterfield, Aristotle argued that a falling body accelerated because it grew more jubilant as it found itself nearer home, and later authorities supposed that a projectile was carried forward by an impetus, sometimes called an "impetuosity." All this was eventually abandoned, and to good effect, but the behavioral sciences still appeal to comparable internal states. No one is surprised to hear it said that a person carrying good news walks more rapidly because he feels jubilant, or acts carelessly because of his impetuosity, or holds stubbornly to a course of action through sheer force of will. Careless references to purpose are still to be found in both physics and biology, but good practice has no place for them; yet almost everyone attributes human behavior to intentions, purposes, aims, and goals. If it is still possible to ask whether a machine can show purpose, the question implies, significantly, that if it can it will more closely resemble a man.

Physics and biology moved farther away from personified causes when they began to attribute the behavior of things to essences, qualities, or natures. To the medieval alchemist, for example, some of the properties of a substance might be due to the mercurial essence, and substances were compared in what might have been called a "chemistry of individual differences." Newton complained of the practice in his contemporaries: "To tell us that every species of thing is endowed with an occult specific quality by which it acts and produces manifest effects is to tell us nothing." (Occult qualities were examples of the hypotheses Newton rejected when he said "Hypotheses non fingo," though he was not quite as good as his word.) Biology continued for a long time to appeal to the *nature* of living things, and it did not wholly abandon vital forces until the twentieth century. Behavior, however, is still attributed to human nature, and there is an extensive "psychology of individual differences" in which people are compared and described in terms of traits of character, capacities, and abilities.

Almost everyone who is concerned with human affairs—as political scientist, philosopher, man of letters, economist, psychologist, linguist, sociologist, theologian, anthropologist, educator, or psychotherapist—continues to talk about human behavior in this prescientific way. Every issue of a daily paper, every magazine, every professional journal, every book with any bearing whatsoever on human behavior will supply examples. We are told that to control the number of people in the world we need to change *attitudes* toward children, overcome *pride* in size of family or in sexual potency, build some *sense of responsibilty* toward offspring, and reduce the role played by a large family in allaying *concern* for old age. To work for peace we must deal with the *will to power* or the *paranoid delusions* of leaders; we must remember that wars begin in the *minds* of men, that there is something suicidal in man—a *death instinct* perhaps—which leads to war, and that man is aggressive by *nature*. To solve the problems of the poor we must inspire *self-respect*, encourage *initiative*, and reduce *frustration*. To allay the disaffection of the young we must provide a *sense of purpose* and reduce feelings of *alienation* or *hope-lessness*. Realizing that we have no effective means of doing any of this, we ourselves may experience *a crisis of belief* or a *loss of confidence*, which can be corrected only by returning to a *faith in man's inner capacities*. This is staple fare. Almost no one questions it. Yet there is nothing like it in modern physics or most of biology, and that fact may well explain why a science and a technology of behavior have been so long delayed.

It is usually supposed that the "behavioristic" objection to ideas, feelings, traits of character, will, and so on concerns the stuff of which they are said to be made. Certain stubborn questions about the nature of mind have, of course, been debated for more than twenty-five hundred years and still go unanswered. How, for example, can the mind move the body? As late as 1965 Karl Popper could put the question this way: "What we want is to understand how such nonphysical things as *purposes, deliberations, plans, decisions, theories, tensions,* and *values* can play a part in bringing about physical changes in the physical world." And, of course, we also want to know where these nonphysical things come from. To that question the Greeks had a simple answer: from the gods. As Dodds has pointed out, the Greeks believed that if a man behaved foolishly, it was because a hostile god had planted $\alpha\tau\eta$ (infatuation) in his breast. A friendly god might give a warrior an extra amount of $\mu\epsilon\nu\sigma$, with the help of which he would fight brilliantly. Aristotle thought there was something divine in thought, and Zeno held that the intellect *was* God.

We cannot take that line today, and the commonest alternative is to appeal to antecedent physical events. A person's genetic endowment, a product of the evolution of the species, is said to explain part of the workings of his mind and his personal history the rest. For example, because of (physical) competition during the course of evolution people now have (nonphysical) feelings of aggression which lead to (physical) acts of hostility. Or, the (physical) punishment a small child receives when he engages in sex play produces (nonphysical) feelings of anxiety which interfere with his (physical) sexual behavior as an adult. The nonphysical stage obviously bridges long periods of time: aggression reaches back into millions of years of evolutionary history, and anxiety acquired when one is a child survives into old age.

The problem of getting from one kind of stuff to another could be avoided if everything were either mental or physical, and both these possibilities have been considered. Some philosophers have tried to stay within the world of the mind, arguing that only immediate experience is real, and experimental psychology began as an attempt to discover the mental laws which governed interactions among mental elements. Contemporary "intrapsychic" theories of psychotherapy tell us how one feeling leads to another (how frustration breeds aggression, for example), how feelings interact, and how feelings which have been put out of mind fight their way back in. The complementary line that the mental stage is really physical was taken, curiously enough, by Freud, who believed that physiology would eventually explain the workings of the mental apparatus. In a similar vein, many physiological psychologists continue to talk freely about states of mind, feelings, and so on, in the belief that it is only a matter of time before we shall understand their physical nature.

The dimensions of the world of mind and the transition from one world to another do raise embarrassing problems, but it is usually possible to ignore them, and this may be good strategy, for the important objection to mentalism is of a very different sort. The world of the mind steals the show. Behavior is not recognized as a subject in its own right. In psychotherapy, for example, the disturbing things a person does or says are almost always regarded merely as symptoms, and compared with the fascinating dramas which are staged in the depths of the mind, behavior itself seems superficial indeed. In linguistics and literary criticism what a man says is almost always treated as the expression of ideas or feelings. In political science, theology, and economics, behavior is usually regarded as the material from which one infers attitudes, intentions, needs, and so on. For more than twenty-five hundred years close attention has been paid to mental life, but only recently has any effort been made to study human behavior as something more than a mere by-product.

The conditions of which behavior is a function are also neglected. The mental explanation brings curiosity to an end. We see the effect in casual discourse. If we ask someone, "Why did you go to the theater?" and he says, "Because I felt like going," we are apt to take his reply as a kind of explanation. It would be much more to the point to know what has happened when he has gone to the theater in the past, what he heard or read about the play he went to see, and what other things in his past or present environments might have induced him to go (as opposed to doing something else), but we accept "I felt like going" as a sort of summary of all this and are not likely to ask for details.

The professional psychologist often stops at the same point. A long time ago William James corrected a prevailing view of the relation between feelings and action by asserting, for example, that we do not run away because we are afraid but are afraid because we run away. In other words, what we feel when we feel afraid is our behavior—the very behavior which in the traditional view expresses the feeling and is explained by it. But how many of those who have considered James's argument have noted that no antecedent event has in fact been pointed out? Neither "because" should be taken seriously. No explanation has been given as to why we run away *and* feel afraid.

Whether we regard ourselves as explaining feelings or the behavior said to be caused by feelings, we give very little attention to antecedent circumstances. The psychotherapist learns about the early life of his patient almost exclusively from the patient's memories, which are known to be unreliable, and he may even argue that what is important is not what actually happened but what the patient remembers. In the psychoanalytic literature there must be at least a hundred references to felt anxiety for every reference to a punishing episode to which anxiety might be traced. We even seem to prefer antecedent histories which are clearly out of reach. There is a good deal of current interest, for example, in what must have happened during the evolution of the species to explain human behavior, and we seem to speak with special confidence just because what actually happened can only be inferred.

Unable to understand how or why the person we see behaves as he does, we attribute his behavior to a person we cannot see, whose behavior we cannot explain either but about whom we are not inclined to ask questions. We probably adopt this strategy not so much because of any lack of interest or power but because of a longstanding conviction that for much of human behavior there *are* no relevant antecedents. The function of the inner man is to provide an explanation which will not be explained in turn. Explanation stops with him. He is not a mediator between past history

and current behavior, he is a *center* from which behavior emanates. He initiates, originates, and creates,
and in doing so he remains, as he was for the Greeks,
divine. We say that he is autonomous—and, so far as a
science of behavior is concerned, that means miraculous.

The position is, of course, vulnerable. Autonomous
man serves to explain only the things we are not yet
able to explain in other ways. His existence depends
upon our ignorance, and he naturally loses status as
we come to know more about behavior. The task of a
scientific analysis is to explain how the behavior of a
person as a physical system is related to the conditions
under which the human species evolved and the conditions under which the individual lives. Unless there
is indeed some capricious or creative intervention,
these events must be related, and no intervention is
in fact needed. The contingencies of survival responsible for man's genetic endowment would produce
tendencies to *act* aggressively, not feelings of aggression. The punishment of sexual behavior changes sexual *behavior*, and any feelings which may arise are at
best by-products. Our age is not suffering from anxiety
but from the accidents, crimes, wars, and other dangerous and painful things to which people are so often
exposed. Young people drop out of school, refuse to
get jobs, and associate only with others of their own
age not because they feel alienated but because of
defective social environments in homes, schools, fac-
tories, and elsewhere.

We can follow the path taken by physics and biology
by turning directly to the relation between behavior
and the environment and neglecting supposed medi-
ating states of mind. Physics did not advance by looking more closely at the jubilance of a falling body, or
biology by looking at the nature of vital spirits, and
we do not need to try to discover what personalities,

states of mind, feelings, traits of character, plans, purposes, intentions, or the other perquisites of autonomous man really are in order to get on with a scientific analysis of behavior.

There are reasons why it has taken us so long to reach this point. The things studied by physics and biology do not behave very much like people, and it eventually seems rather ridiculous to speak of the jubilance of a falling body or the impetuosity of a projectile; but people do behave like people, and the outer man whose behavior is to be explained could be very much like the inner man whose behavior is said to explain it. The inner man has been created in the image of the outer.

A more important reason is that the inner man seems at times to be directly observed. We must infer the jubilance of a falling body, but can we not *feel* our own jubilance? We do, indeed, feel things inside our own skin, but we do not feel the things which have been invented to explain behavior. The possessed man does not feel the possessing *demon* and may even deny that one exists. The juvenile delinquent does not feel his *disturbed personality*. The intelligent man does not feel his *intelligence* or the introvert his *introversion*. (In fact, these dimensions of mind or character are said to be observable only through complex statistical procedures.) The speaker does not feel the *grammatical* rules he is said to apply in composing sentences, and men spoke grammatically for thousands of years before anyone knew there were rules. The respondent to a questionnaire does not feel the *attitudes* or *opinions* which lead him to check items in particular ways. We do feel certain states of our bodies associated with behavior, but as Freud pointed out, we behave in the same way when we do not feel them; they are by-products and not to be mistaken for causes.

There is a much more important reason why we have been so slow in discarding mentalistic explanations: it has been hard to find alternatives. Presumably we must look for them in the external environment, but the role of the environment is by no means clear. The history of the theory of evolution illustrates the problem. Before the nineteenth century, the environment was thought of simply as a passive setting in which many different kinds of organisms were born, reproduced themselves, and died. No one saw that the environment was responsible for the fact that there *were* many different kinds (and that fact, significantly enough, was attributed to a creative Mind). The trouble was that the environment acts in an inconspicuous way: it does not push or pull, it *selects*. For thousands of years in the history of human thought the process of natural selection went unseen in spite of its extraordinary importance. When it was eventually discovered, it became, of course, the key to evolutionary theory.

The effect of the environment on behavior remained obscure for an even longer time. We can see what organisms do to the world around them, as they take from it what they need and ward off its dangers, but it is much harder to see what the world does to them. It was Descartes who first suggested that the environment might play an active role in the determination of behavior, and he was apparently able to do so only because he was given a strong hint. He knew about certain automata in the Royal Gardens of France which were operated hydraulically by concealed valves. As Descartes described it, people entering the gardens "necessarily tread on certain tiles or plates, which are so disposed that if they approach a bathing Diana, they cause her to hide in the rose-bushes, and if they try to follow her, they cause a Neptune to come forward to meet them, threatening them with his trident." The figures were entertaining just because they behaved like people, and it appeared, therefore, that something very much like human behavior could be explained mechanically. Descartes took the hint: living organisms might move for similar reasons. (He excluded the human organism, presumably to avoid religious controversy.)

The triggering action of the environment came to be called a "stimulus"—the Latin for goad—and the effect on an organism a "response," and together they were said to compose a "reflex." Reflexes were first demonstrated in small decapitated animals, such as salamanders, and it is significant that the principle was challenged throughout the nineteenth century because it seemed to deny the existence of an autonomous agent—the "soul of the spinal cord"—to which movement of a decapitated body had been attributed. When Pavlov showed how new reflexes could be built up through conditioning, a full-fledged stimulus-response psychology was born, in which all behavior was regarded as reactions to stimuli. One writer put it this way: "We are prodded or lashed through life." The stimulus-response model was never very convincing, however, and it did not solve the basic problem, because something like an inner man had to be invented to convert a stimulus into a response. Information theory ran into the same problem when an inner "processer" had to be invented to convert input into output.

The effect of an eliciting stimulus is relatively easy to see, and it is not surprising that Descartes' hypothesis held a dominant position in behavior theory for a long time, but it was a false scent from which a scientific analysis is only now recovering. The environment not only prods or lashes, it *selects*. Its role is similar to that in natural selection, though on a very different time scale, and was overlooked for the same reason. It is now clear that we must take into account what the environment does to an organism not only before but after it responds. Behavior is shaped and maintained by its consequences. Once this fact is recognized, we can formulate the interaction between organism and environment in a much more comprehensive way.

There are two important results. One concerns the basic analysis. Behavior which operates upon the environment to produce consequences ("operant" behavior) can be studied by arranging environments in which specific consequences are contingent upon it. The contingencies under investigation have become steadily more complex, and one by one they are taking over the explanatory functions previously assigned to personalities, states of mind, feelings, traits of character, purposes, and intentions. The second result is practical: the environment can be manipulated. It is true that man's genetic endowment can be changed only very slowly, but changes in the environment of the individual have quick and dramatic effects. A technology of operant behavior is, as we shall see, already well advanced, and it may prove to be commensurate with our problems.

That possibility raises another problem, however, which must be solved if we are to take advantage of our gains. We have moved forward by dispossessing autonomous man, but he has not departed gracefully. He is conducting a sort of rear-guard action in which, unfortunately, he can marshal formidable support. He is still an important figure in political science, law, religion, economics, anthropology, sociology, psychotherapy, philosophy, ethics, history, education, child care, linguistics, architecture, city planning, and family life. These fields have their specialists, and every specialist has a theory, and in almost every theory the autonomy of the individual is unquestioned. The inner man is not seriously threatened by data obtained through casual observation or from studies of the structure of behavior, and many of these fields deal only with groups of people, where statistical or actuarial data impose few restraints upon the individual. The result is a tremendous weight of traditional "knowledge," which must be corrected or displaced by a scientific analysis.

Two features of autonomous man are particularly troublesome. In the traditional view, a person is free. He is autonomous in the sense that his behavior is uncaused. He can therefore be held responsible for what he does and justly punished if he offends. That view, together with its associated practices, must be re-examined when a scientific analysis reveals unsuspected controlling relations between behavior and environment. A certain amount of external control can be tolerated. Theologians have accepted the fact that man must be predestined to do what an omniscient God knows he will do, and the Greek dramatist took inexorable fate as his favorite theme. Soothsayers and astrologers often claim to predict what men will do, and they have always been in demand. Biographers and historians have searched for "influences" in the lives of individuals and peoples. Folk wisdom and the insights of essayists like Montaigne and Bacon imply some kind of predictability in human conduct, and the statistical and actuarial evidences of the social sciences point in the same direction.

Autonomous man survives in the face of all this be-

cause he is the happy exception. Theologians have
reconciled predestination with free will, and the Greek
audience, moved by the portrayal of an inescapable
destiny, walked out of the theater free men. The
course of history has been turned by the death of a
leader or a storm at sea, as a life has been changed
by a teacher or a love affair, but these things do not
happen to everyone, and they do not affect everyone
in the same way. Some historians have made a virtue
of the unpredictability of history. Actuarial evidence
is easily ignored; we read that hundreds of people
will be killed in traffic accidents on a holiday weekend
and take to the road as if personally exempt. Very
little behavioral science raises "the specter of predict-
able man." On the contrary, many anthropologists,
sociologists, and psychologists have used their expert
knowledge to prove that man is free, purposeful, and
responsible. Freud was a determinist—on faith, if not
on the evidence—but many Freudians have no hesi-
tation in assuring their patients that they are free to
choose among different courses of action and are in
the long run the architects of their own destinies.

This escape route is slowly closed as new evidences of
the predictability of human behavior are discovered.
Personal exemption from a complete determinism
is revoked as a scientific analysis progresses, particularly in accounting for the behavior of the individual. Joseph Wood Krutch has acknowledged the actuarial facts while insisting on personal freedom: "We
can predict with a considerable degree of accuracy
how many people will go to the seashore on a day
when the temperature reaches a certain point, even
how many will jump off a bridge . . . although I am
not, nor are you, compelled to do either." But he can
scarcely mean that those who go to the seashore do
not go for good reason, or that circumstances in the

life of a suicide do not have some bearing on the fact that he jumps off a bridge. The distinction is tenable only so long as a word like "compel" suggests a particularly conspicuous and forcible mode of control. A scientific analysis naturally moves in the direction of clarifying all kinds of controlling relations.

By questioning the control exercised by autonomous man and demonstrating the control exercised by the environment, a science of behavior also seems to question dignity or worth. A person is responsible for his behavior, not only in the sense that he may be justly blamed or punished when he behaves badly, but also in the sense that he is to be given credit and admired for his achievements. A scientific analysis shifts the credit as well as the blame to the environment, and traditional practices can then no longer be justified. These are sweeping changes, and those who are committed to traditional theories and practices naturally resist them.

There is a third source of trouble. As the emphasis shifts to the environment, the individual seems to be exposed to a new kind of danger. Who is to construct the controlling environment and to what end? Autonomous man presumably controls himself in accordance with a built-in set of values; he works for what he finds good. But what will the putative controller find good, and will it be good for those he controls? Answers to questions of this sort are said, of course, to call for value judgments.

Freedom, dignity, and value are major issues, and unfortunately they become more crucial as the power of a technology of behavior becomes more nearly commensurate with the problems to be solved. The very change which has brought some hope of a solution is responsible for a growing opposition to the kind of solution proposed. This conflict is itself a problem in human behavior and may be approached as such. A science of behavior is by no means as far advanced as physics or biology, but it has an advantage in that it may throw some light on its own difficulties. Science *is* human behavior, and so is the opposition to science. What has happened in man's struggle for freedom and dignity, and what problems arise when scientific knowledge begins to be relevant in that struggle? Answers to these questions may help to clear the way for the technology we so badly need.

In what follows, these issues are discussed "from a scientific point of view," but this does not mean that the reader will need to know the details of a scientific analysis of behavior. A mere interpretation will suffice. The nature of such an interpretation is, however, easily misunderstood. We often talk about things we cannot observe or measure with the precision demanded by a scientific analysis, and in doing so there is much to be gained from using terms and principles which have been worked out under more precise conditions. The sea at dusk glows with a strange light, frost forms on the windowpane in an unusual pattern, and the soup fails to thicken on the stove, and specialists tell us why. We can, of course, challenge them: they do not have "the facts," and what they say cannot be "proved," but they are nevertheless more likely to be right than those who lack an experimental background, and they alone can tell us how to move on to a more precise study if it seems worthwhile.

An experimental analysis of behavior offers similar advantages. When we have observed behavioral processes under controlled conditions, we can more easily spot them in the world at large. We can identify significant features of behavior and of the environment and are therefore able to neglect insignificant ones, no matter how fascinating they may be. We can reject traditional explanations if they have been tried and found wanting in an experimental analysis and then press forward in our inquiry with unallayed curiosity. The instances of behavior cited in what follows are not offered as "proof" of the interpretation. The proof is to be found in the basic analysis. The principles used in interpreting the instances have a plausibility which would be lacking in principles drawn entirely from casual observation.

The text will often seem inconsistent. English, like all languages, is full of prescientific terms which usually suffice for purposes of casual discourse. No one looks askance at the astronomer when he says that the sun rises or that the stars come out at night, for it would be ridiculous to insist that he should always say that the sun appears over the horizon as the earth turns or that the stars become visible as the atmosphere ceases to refract sunlight. All we ask is that he can give a more precise translation if one is needed. The English language contains many more expressions referring to human behavior than to other aspects of the world, and technical alternatives are much less familiar. The use of casual expressions is therefore much more likely to be challenged. It may seem inconsistent to ask the reader to "keep a point in mind" when he has been told that mind is an explanatory fiction, or to "consider the idea of freedom" if an idea is simply an imagined precursor of behavior, or to speak of "reassuring those who fear a science of behavior" when all that is meant is changing their behavior with respect to such a science. The book could have been written for a technical reader without expressions of that sort, but the issues are important to the nonspecialist and need to be discussed in a nontechnical fashion. No doubt many of the mentalistic

expressions imbedded in the English language cannot
be as rigorously translated as "sunrise," but acceptable
translations are not out of reach.

* * *

Almost all our major problems involve human behavior, and they cannot be solved by physical and
biological technology alone. What is needed is a technology of behavior, but we have been slow to develop
the science from which such a technology might be
drawn. One difficulty is that almost all of what is
called behavioral science continues to trace behavior
to states of mind, feelings, traits of character, human
nature, and so on. Physics and biology once followed
similar practices and advanced only when they dis-
carded them. The behavioral sciences have been slow
to change partly because the explanatory entities often
seem to be directly observed and partly because other
kinds of explanations have been hard to find. The
environment is obviously important, but its role has
remained obscure. It does not push or pull, it *selects*,
and this function is difficult to discover and analyze.
The role of natural selection in evolution was formulated only a little more than a hundred years ago, and
the selective role of the environment in shaping and
maintaining the behavior of the individual is only beginning to be recognized and studied. As the interaction between organism and environment has come
to be understood, however, effects once assigned to
states of mind, feelings, and traits are beginning to be
traced to accessible conditions, and a technology of
behavior may therefore become available. It will not
solve our problems, however, until it replaces traditional prescientific views, and these are strongly en-
trenched. Freedom and dignity illustrate the difficulty.
They are the possessions of the autonomous man of

traditional theory, and they are essential to practices in which a person is held responsible for his conduct and given credit for his achievements. A scientific analysis shifts both the responsibility and the achievement to the environment. It also raises questions concerning "values." Who will use a technology and to what ends? Until these issues are resolved, a technology of behavior will continue to be rejected, and with it possibly the only way to solve our problems.

2
Freedom

ALMOST ALL LIVING THINGS act to free themselves from harmful contacts. A kind of freedom is achieved by the relatively simple forms of behavior called reflexes. A person sneezes and frees his respiratory passages from irritating substances. He vomits and frees his stomach from indigestible or poisonous food. He pulls back his hand and frees it from a sharp or hot object. More elaborate forms of behavior have similar effects. When confined, people struggle ("in rage") and break free. When in danger they flee from or attack its source. Behavior of this kind presumably evolved because of its survival value; it is as much a part of what we call the human genetic endowment as breathing, sweating, or digesting food. And through conditioning similiar behavior may be acquired with respect to novel objects which could have played no role in evolution. These are no doubt minor instances of the struggle to be free, but they are significant. We do not attribute them to any love of freedom; they are simply forms of behavior which have proved useful in reducing various threats to the individual and hence to the species in the course of evolution.

* * *

A much more important role is played by behavior which weakens harmful stimuli in another way. It is not acquired in the form of conditioned reflexes, but as the product of a different process called operant conditioning. When a bit of behavior is followed by a certain kind of consequence, it is more likely to occur again, and a consequence having this effect is called a reinforcer. Food, for example, is a reinforcer to a hungry organism; anything the organism does that is followed by the receipt of food is more likely to be done again whenever the organism is hungry. Some stimuli are called negative reinforcers; any response which reduces the intensity of such a stimulus—or ends it—is more likely to be emitted when the stimulus recurs. Thus, if a person escapes from a hot sun when he moves under cover, he is more likely to move under cover when the sun is again hot. The reduction in temperature reinforces the behavior it is "contingent upon"—that is, the behavior it follows. Operant conditioning also occurs when a person simply avoids a hot sun—when, roughly speaking, he escapes from the *threat* of a hot sun.

Negative reinforcers are called aversive in the sense that they are the things organisms "turn away from." The term suggests a spatial separation—moving or running away from something—but the essential relation is temporal. In a standard apparatus used to study the process in the laboratory, an arbitrary response simply weakens an aversive stimulus or brings it to an end. A great deal of physical technology is the result of this kind of struggle for freedom. Over the centuries, in erratic ways, men have constructed a world in which they are relatively free of many kinds of threatening or harmful stimuli—extremes of temperature, sources of infection, hard labor, danger, and even those minor aversive stimuli called discomfort.

Escape and avoidance play a much more important role in the struggle for freedom when the aversive conditions are generated by other people. Other people

can be aversive without, so to speak, trying: they can
be rude, dangerous, contagious, or annoying, and one
escapes from them or avoids them accordingly. They
may also be "intentionally" aversive—that is, they may
treat other people aversively because of what follows.
Thus, a slave driver induces a slave to work by whipping him when he stops; by resuming work the slave
escapes from the whipping (and incidentally reinforces
the slave driver's behavior in using the whip). A parent nags a child until the child performs a task; by
performing the task the child escapes nagging (and
reinforces the parent's behavior). The blackmailer
threatens exposure unless the victim pays; by paying,
the victim escapes from the threat (and reinforces the
practice). A teacher threatens corporal punishment or
failure until his students pay attention; by paying attention the students escape from the threat of punishment (and reinforce the teacher for threatening it).
In one form or another intentional aversive control is
the pattern of most social coordination—in ethics, religion, government, economics, education, psychotherapy, and family life.

A person escapes from or avoids aversive treatment
by behaving in ways which reinforce those who treated
him aversively until he did so, but he may escape in
other ways. For example, he may simply move out of
range. A person may escape from slavery, emigrate or
defect from a government, desert from an army, become an apostate from a religion, play truant, leave
home, or drop out of a culture as a hobo, hermit, or
hippie. Such behavior is as much a product of the aversive conditions as the behavior the conditions were
designed to evoke. The latter can be guaranteed only
by sharpening the contingencies or by using stronger
aversive stimuli.

Another anomalous mode of escape is to attack those

who arrange aversive conditions and weaken or destroy their power. We may attack those who crowd us or annoy us, as we attack the weeds in our garden, but again the struggle for freedom is mainly directed toward intentional controllers—toward those who treat others aversively in order to induce them to behave in particular ways. Thus, a child may stand up to his parents, a citizen may overthrow a government, a communicant may reform a religion, a student may attack a teacher or vandalize a school, and a dropout may work to destroy a culture.

It is possible that man's genetic endowment supports this kind of struggle for freedom: when treated aversively people tend to act aggressively or to be reinforced by signs of having worked aggressive damage. Both tendencies should have had evolutionary advantages, and they can easily be demonstrated. If two organisms which have been coexisting peacefully receive painful shocks, they immediately exhibit characteristic patterns of aggression toward each other. The aggressive behavior is not necessarily directed toward the actual source of stimulation; it may be "displaced" toward any convenient person or object. Vandalism and riots are often forms of undirected or misdirected aggression. An organism which has received a painful shock will also, if possible, act to gain access to another organism toward which it can act aggressively. The extent to which human aggression exemplifies innate tendencies is not clear, and many of the ways in which people attack and thus weaken or destroy the power of intentional controllers are quite obviously learned.

What we may call the "literature of freedom" has been designed to induce people to escape from or attack those who act to control them aversively. The content of the literature is the philosophy of freedom, but philosophies are among those inner causes which need to be scrutinized. We say that a person behaves in a given way because he possesses a philosophy, but we infer the philosophy from the behavior and therefore cannot use it in any satisfactory way as an explanation, at least until it is in turn explained. The literature of freedom, on the other hand, has a simple objective status. It consists of books, pamphlets, manifestoes, speeches, and other verbal products, designed to induce people to act to free themselves from various kinds of intentional control. It does not impart a philosophy of freedom; it induces people to act.

The literature often emphasizes the aversive conditions under which people live, perhaps by contrasting them with conditions in a freer world. It thus makes the conditions more aversive, "increasing the misery" of those it is trying to rescue. It also identifies those from whom one is to escape or those whose power is to be weakened through attack. Characteristic villains of the literature are tyrants, priests, generals, capitalists, martinet teachers, and domineering parents.

The literature also prescribes modes of action. It has not been much concerned with escape, possibly because advice has not been needed; instead, it has emphasized how controlling power may be weakened or destroyed. Tyrants are to be overthrown, ostracized, or assassinated. The legitimacy of a government is to be questioned. The ability of a religious agency to mediate supernatural sanctions is to be challenged. Strikes and boycotts are to be organized to weaken the economic power which supports aversive practices. The argument is strengthened by exhorting people to act, describing likely results, reviewing successful instances on the model of the advertising testimonial, and so on.

The would-be controllers do not, of course, remain

inactive. Governments make escape impossible by banning travel or severely punishing or incarcerating defectors. They keep weapons and other sources of power out of the hands of revolutionaries. They destroy the written literature of freedom and imprison or kill those who carry it orally. If the struggle for freedom is to succeed, it must then be intensified.

The importance of the literature of freedom can scarcely be questioned. Without help or guidance people submit to aversive conditions in the most surprising way. This is true even when the aversive conditions are part of the natural environment. Darwin observed, for example, that the Fuegians seemed to make no effort to protect themselves from the cold; they wore only scant clothing and made little use of it against the weather. And one of the most striking things about the struggle for freedom from intentional control is how often it has been lacking. Many people have submitted to the most obvious religious, governmental, and economic controls for centuries, striking for freedom only sporadically, if at all. The literature of freedom has made an essential contribution to the elimination of many aversive practices in government, religion, education, family life, and the production of goods.

The contributions of the literature of freedom, however, are not usually described in these terms. Some traditional theories could conceivably be said to define freedom as the absence of aversive control, but the emphasis has been on how that condition *feels*. Other traditional theories could conceivably be said to define freedom as a person's condition when he is behaving under nonaversive control, but the emphasis has been upon a state of mind associated with doing what one wants. According to John Stuart Mill, "Liberty consists in doing what one desires." The literature of freedom has been important in changing practice (it has changed

practices whenever it has had any effect whatsoever),
but it has nevertheless defined its task as the changing
of states of mind and feelings. Freedom is a "possession." A person escapes from or destroys the power of
a controller in order to feel free, and once he feels
free and can do what he desires, no further action is
recommended and none is prescribed by the literature
of freedom, except perhaps eternal vigilance lest control be resumed.

The feeling of freedom becomes an unreliable guide to
action as soon as would-be controllers turn to nonaversive measures, as they are likely to do to avoid the
problems raised when the controllee escapes or attacks.
Nonaversive measures are not as conspicuous as aversive and are likely to be acquired more slowly, but they
have obvious advantages which promote their use.
Productive labor, for example, was once the result of
punishment: the slave worked to avoid the consequences of not working. Wages exemplify a different
principle; a person is paid when he behaves in a given
way so that he will continue to behave in that way.
Although it has long been recognized that rewards
have useful effects, wage systems have evolved slowly.
In the nineteenth century it was believed that an industrial society required a hungry labor force; wages
would be effective only if the hungry worker could
exchange them for food. By making labor less aversive
—for instance, by shortening hours and improving conditions—it has been possible to get men to work for
lesser rewards. Until recently teaching was almost
entirely aversive: the student studied to escape the
consequences of not studying, but nonaversive techniques are gradually being discovered and used. The
skillful parent learns to reward a child for good behavior rather than punish him for bad. Religious

agencies move from the threat of hellfire to an emphasis on God's love, and governments turn from aversive sanctions to various kinds of inducements, as we shall note again shortly. What the layman calls a reward is a "positive reinforcer," the effects of which have been exhaustively studied in the experimental analysis of operant behavior. The effects are not as easily recognized as those of aversive contingencies because they tend to be deferred, and applications have therefore been delayed, but techniques as powerful as the older aversive techniques are now available.

A problem arises for the defender of freedom when the behavior generated by positive reinforcement has deferred aversive consequences. This is particularly likely to be the case when the process is used in intentional control, where the gain to the controller usually means a loss to the controllee. What are called conditioned positive reinforcers can often be used with deferred aversive results. Money is an example. It is reinforcing only after it has been exchanged for reinforcing things, but it can be used as a reinforcer when exchange is impossible. A counterfeit bill, a bad check, a stopped check, or an unkept promise are conditioned reinforcers, although aversive consequences are usually quickly discovered. The archetypal pattern is the gold brick. Countercontrol quickly follows: we escape from or attack those who misuse conditioned reinforcers in this way. But the misuse of many social reinforcers often goes unnoticed. Personal attention, approval, and affection are usually reinforcing only if there has been some connection with already effective reinforcers, but they can be used when a connection is lacking. The simulated approval and affection with which parents and teachers are often urged to solve behavior problems are counterfeit. So are flattery, backslapping, and many other ways of "winning friends."

Genuine reinforcers can be used in ways which have aversive consequences. A government may prevent defection by making life more interesting—by providing bread and circuses and by encouraging sports, gambling, the use of alcohol and other drugs, and various kinds of sexual behavior, where the effect is to keep people within reach of aversive sanctions. The Goncourt brothers noted the rise of pornography in the France of their day: "Pornographic literature," they wrote, "serves a Bas-Empire . . . one tames a people as one tames lions, by masturbation."

Genuine positive reinforcement can also be misused because the sheer quantity of reinforcers is not proportional to the effect on behavior. Reinforcement is usually only intermittent, and the schedule of reinforcement is more important than the amount received. Certain schedules generate a great deal of behavior in return for very little reinforcement, and the possibility has naturally not been overlooked by would-be controllers. Two examples of schedules which are easily used to the disadvantage of those reinforced may be noted.

In the incentive system known as piece-work pay, the worker is paid a given amount for each unit of work performed. The system seems to guarantee a balance between the goods produced and the money received. The schedule is attractive to management, which can calculate labor costs in advance, and also to the worker, who can control the amount he earns. This so-called "fixed-ratio" schedule of reinforcement can, however, be used to generate a great deal of behavior for very little return. It induces the worker to work fast, and the ratio can then be "stretched"—that is, more work can be demanded for each unit of pay without running the risk that the worker will stop working. His ultimate condition—hard work with very little pay—may be acutely aversive.

A related schedule, called variable-ratio, is at the heart of all gambling systems. A gambling enterprise pays people for giving it money—that is, it pays them when they make bets. But it pays on a kind of schedule which sustains betting even though, in the long run, the amount paid is less than the amount wagered. At first the mean ratio may be favorable to the bettor; he "wins." But the ratio can be stretched in such a way that he continues to play even when he begins to lose. The stretching may be accidental (an early run of good luck which grows steadily worse may create a dedicated gambler), or the ratio may be deliberately stretched by someone who controls the odds. In the long run the "utility" is negative: the gambler loses all.

It is difficult to deal effectively with deferred aversive consequences because they do not occur at a time when escape or attack is feasible—when, for example, the controller can be identified or is within reach. But the immediate reinforcement is positive and goes unchallenged. The problem to be solved by those who are concerned with freedom is to create immediate aversive consequences. A classical problem concerns "self-control." A person eats too much and gets sick but survives to eat too much again. Delicious food or the behavior evoked by it must be made sufficiently aversive so that a person will "escape from it" by not eating it. (It might be thought that he can escape from it only before eating it, but the Romans escaped afterward through the use of a vomitorium.) Current aversive stimuli may be conditioned. Something of the sort is done when eating too much is called wrong, gluttonous, or sinful. Other kinds of behavior to be suppressed may be declared illegal and punished accordingly. The more deferred the aversive consequences the greater the problem. It has taken a great deal of "engineering" to bring the ultimate consequences of smoking cigarettes to bear on the behavior. A fascinating hobby, a sport, a love affair, or a large salary may compete with activities which would be more reinforcing in the long run, but the run is too long to make countercontrol possible. That is why countercontrol is exerted, if at all, only by those who suffer aversive consequences but are not subject to positive reinforcement. Laws are passed against gambling, unions oppose piece-work pay, and no one is allowed to pay young children to work for them or to pay anyone for engaging in immoral behavior, but these measures may be strongly opposed by those whom they are designed to protect. The gambler objects to antigambling laws and the alcoholic to any kind of prohibition; and a child or prostitute may be willing to work for what is offered.

The literature of freedom has never come to grips with techniques of control which do not generate escape or counterattack because it has dealt with the problem in terms of states of mind and feelings. In his book *Sovereignty,* Bertrand de Jouvenel quotes two important figures in that literature. According to Leibnitz, "Liberty consists in the power to do what one wants to do," and according to Voltaire, "When I can do what I want to do, there is my liberty for me." But both writers add a concluding phrase: Leibnitz, ". . . or in the power to want what can be got," and Voltaire, more candidly, ". . . but I can't help wanting what I do want." Jouvenel relegates these comments to a footnote, saying that the power to want is a matter of "interior liberty" (the freedom of the inner man!) which falls outside the "gambit of freedom."

A person wants something if he acts to get it when the occasion arises. A person who says "I want something to eat" will presumably eat when something becomes available. If he says "I want to get warm," he will presumably move into a warm place when he can. These acts have been reinforced in the past by whatever was wanted. What a person *feels* when he feels himself wanting something depends upon the circumstances. Food is reinforcing only in a state of deprivation, and a person who wants something to eat may feel parts of that state—for example, hunger pangs. A person who wants to get warm presumably feels cold. Conditions associated with a high probability of responding may also be felt, together with aspects of the present occasion which are similar to those of past occasions upon which behavior has been reinforced. Wanting is not, however, a feeling, nor is a feeling the reason a person acts to get what he wants. Certain contingencies have raised the probability of behavior and at the same time have created conditions which may be felt. Freedom is a matter of contingencies of reinforcement, not of the feelings the contingencies generate. The distinction is particularly important when the contingencies do not generate escape or counter-attack.

The uncertainty which surrounds the countercontrol of nonaversive measures is easily exemplified. In the 1930's it seemed necessary to cut agricultural production. The Agricultural Adjustment Act authorized the Secretary of Agriculture to make "rental or benefit payments" to farmers who agreed to produce less—to pay the farmers, in fact, what they would have made on the food they agreed not to produce. It would have been unconstitutional to *compel* them to reduce production, but the government argued that it was merely inviting them to do so. But the Supreme Court recognized that positive inducement can be as irresistible as aversive measures when it ruled that "the power to confer or withhold unlimited benefit is the power to coerce or destroy." The decision was later reversed, however, when the Court ruled that "to hold that motive or temptation is equivalent to coercion is to plunge the law into endless difficulties." We are considering some of these difficulties.

The same issue arises when a government runs a lottery in order to raise revenue to reduce taxes. The government takes the same amount of money from its citizens in both cases, though not necessarily from the same citizens. By running a lottery it avoids certain unwanted consequences: people escape from heavy taxation by moving away or they counterattack by throwing a government which imposes new taxes out of office. A lottery, taking advantage of a stretched variable-ratio schedule of reinforcement, has neither of these effects. The only opposition comes from those who in general oppose gambling enterprises and who are themselves seldom gamblers.

A third example is the practice of inviting prisoners to volunteer for possibly dangerous experiments—for example, on new drugs—in return for better living conditions or shortened sentences. Everyone would protest if the prisoners were forced to participate, but are they really free when positively reinforced, particularly when the condition to be improved or the sentence to be shortened has been imposed by the state?

The issue often arises in more subtle forms. It has been argued, for example, that uncontrolled contraceptive services and abortion do not "confer unrestricted freedom to reproduce or not to reproduce because they cost time and money." Impoverished members of society should be given compensation if they are to have a truly "free choice." If the just compensation exactly offsets the time and money needed to practice birth control, then people will indeed be free of the control exerted by the loss of time and money, but whether or not they then have children will still depend upon other conditions which have not been specified. If a nation generously reinforces the practices of contraception and abortion, to what extent are its citizens free to have or not to have children?

Uncertainty about positive control is evident in two remarks which often appear in the literature of freedom. It is said that even though behavior is completely determined, it is better that a man "feel free" or "believe that he is free." If this means that it is better to be controlled in ways which have no aversive consequences, we may agree, but if it means that it is better to be controlled in ways against which no one revolts, it fails to take account of the possibility of deferred aversive consequences. A second comment seems more appropriate: "It is better to be a conscious slave than a happy one." The word "slave" clarifies the nature of the ultimate consequences being considered: they are exploitative and hence aversive. What the slave is to be conscious of is his misery; and a system of slavery so well designed that it does not breed revolt is the real threat. The literature of freedom has been designed to make men "conscious" of aversive control, but in its choice of methods it has failed to rescue the happy slave.

One of the great figures in the literature of freedom, Jean-Jacques Rousseau, did not fear the power of positive reinforcement. In his remarkable book *Émile* he gave the following advice to teachers:

Let [the child] believe that he is always in control, though it is always you [the teacher] who really controls. There is no subjugation so perfect as that which keeps the appearance of freedom, for in that way one captures volition itself. The poor baby, knowing nothing, able to do nothing, having learned nothing, is he not at your mercy? Can you not arrange everything in the world which surrounds him? Can you not influence him as you wish? His work, his play, his pleasures, his pains, are not all these in your hands and without his knowing? Doubtless he ought to do only what he wants; but he ought to want to do only what you want him to do; he ought not to take a step which you have not foreseen; he ought not to open his mouth without your knowing what he will say.

Rousseau could take this line because he had unlimited faith in the benevolence of teachers, who would use their absolute control for the good of their students. But, as we shall see later, benevolence is no guarantee against the misuse of power, and very few figures in the history of the struggle for freedom have shown Rousseau's lack of concern. On the contrary, they have taken the extreme position that all control is wrong. In so doing they exemplify a behavioral process called generalization. Many instances of control are aversive, in either their nature or their consequences, and hence all instances are to be avoided. The Puritans carried the generalization a step further by arguing that most positive reinforcement was wrong, whether or not it was intentionally arranged, just because it occasionally got people into trouble.

The literature of freedom has encouraged escape from or attack upon all controllers. It has done so by making any indication of control aversive. Those who manipulate human behavior are said to be evil men, necessarily bent on exploitation. Control is clearly the opposite of freedom, and if freedom is good, control must be bad. What is overlooked is control which does not have aversive consequences at any time. Many social practices essential to the welfare of the species involve the control of one person by another, and no one can suppress them who has any concern for human achievements. We shall see later that in order to maintain the position that all control is wrong, it has been necessary to disguise or conceal the nature of useful practices, to prefer weak practices just because they can be disguised or concealed, and—a most extraordinary result indeed!—to perpetuate punitive measures.

The problem is to free men, not from control, but from certain kinds of control, and it can be solved only if our analysis takes all consequences into account. How people feel about control, before or after the literature of freedom has worked on their feelings, does not lead to useful distinctions.

Were it not for the unwarranted generalization that all control is wrong, we should deal with the social environment as simply as we deal with the nonsocial. Although technology has freed men from certain aversive features of the environment, it has not freed them from the environment. We accept the fact that we depend upon the world around us, and we simply change the nature of the dependency. In the same way, to make the social environment as free as possible of aversive stimuli we do not need to destroy that environment or escape from it; we need to redesign it.

*   *   *

Man's struggle for freedom is not due to a will to be free, but to certain behavioral processes characteristic of the human organism, the chief effect of which is the avoidance of or escape from so-called "aversive" features of the environment. Physical and biological technologies have heen mainly concerned with natural aversive stimuli; the struggle for freedom is concerned with stimuli intentionally arranged by other people. The literature of freedom has identified the other people and has proposed ways of escaping from them or weakening or destroying their power. It has been successful in reducing the aversive stimuli used in intentional control, but it has made the mistake of defining freedom in terms of states of mind or feelings, and it has therefore not been able to deal effectively with techniques of control which do not breed escape or revolt but nevertheless have aversive consequences. It has been forced to brand all control as wrong and to misrepresent many of the advantages to be gained from a social environment. It is unprepared for the next step, which is not to free men from control but to analyze and change the kinds of control to which they are exposed.

3
Dignity

ANY EVIDENCE that a person's behavior may be attributed to external circumstances seems to threaten his dignity or worth. We are not inclined to give a person credit for achievements which are in fact due to forces over which he has no control. We tolerate a certain amount of such evidence, as we accept without alarm some evidence that a man is not free. No one is greatly disturbed when important details of works of art and literature, political careers, and scientific discoveries are attributed to "influences" in the lives of artists, writers, statesmen, and scientists respectively. But as an analysis of behavior adds further evidence, the achievements for which a person himself is to be given credit seem to approach zero, and both the evidence and the science which produces it are then challenged. *environmental control*

Freedom is an issue raised by the aversive consequences of behavior, but dignity concerns positive reinforcement. When someone behaves in a way we find reinforcing, we make him more likely to do so again by praising or commending him. We applaud a performer precisely to induce him to repeat his performance, as the expressions "Again!" "Encore!" and "*Bis!*" indicate. We attest to the value of a person's behavior by patting him on the back, or saying "Good!" or "Right!" or giving him a "token of our esteem" such as a prize, honor, or award. Some of these things are reinforcing in their own right—a pat on the back may be a kind of caress, and prizes include established reinforcers—but others are conditioned—that is, they reinforce only because they have been accompanied by or exchanged for established reinforcers. Praise and approval are generally reinforcing because anyone who praises a person or approves what he has done is inclined to reinforce him in other ways. (The reinforcement may be the reduction of a threat; to approve a draft of a resolution is often simply to cease to object to it.)

There may be a natural inclination to be reinforcing to those who reinforce us, as there seems to be to attack those who attack us, but similar behavior is generated by many social contingencies. We commend those who work for our good because we are reinforced when they continue to do so. When we give a person credit *for* something we identify an additional reinforcing consequence. To give a person credit for winning a game is to emphasize the fact that the victory was contingent on something he did, and the victory may then become more reinforcing to him.

The amount of credit a person receives is related in a curious way to the visibility of the causes of his behavior. We withhold credit when the causes are conspicuous. We do not, for example, ordinarily commend a person for responding reflexly: we do not give him credit for coughing, sneezing, or vomiting even though the result may be valuable. For the same reason we do not give much credit for behavior which is under conspicuous aversive control even though it may be useful. As Montaigne observed, "Whatever is enforced by command is more imputed to him who exacts than to him who performs." We do not commend the groveler even though he may be serving an important function.

Nor do we praise behavior which is traceable to conspicuous positive reinforcement. We share Iago's contempt for the

> . . . duteous and knee-crooking knave
> That, doting on his own obsequious bondage,
> Wears out his time, much like his master's ass,
> For nought but provender . . .

To be excessively controlled by sexual reinforcement is to be "infatuated," and the etymology of the word was memorialized by Kipling in two famous lines: "A fool there was and he made his prayer . . ./To a rag, a bone, and a hank of hair . . ." Members of the leisure classes have generally lost status when they submitted to pecuniary reinforcement by "going into trade." Among those reinforced with money, credit usually varies with the conspicuousness of the reinforcement: it is less commendable to work for a weekly wage than a monthly salary, even though the total income is the same. The loss in status may explain why most professions have come only slowly under economic control. For a long time teachers were not paid, presumably because pay would have been beneath their dignity; and lending money at interest was stigmatized for centuries and even punished as usury. We do not give a writer much credit for a potboiler, or an artist for a picture obviously painted to sell in the current fashion. Above all we do not give credit to those who are conspicuously working for credit.

We give credit generously when there are no obvious reasons for the behavior. Love is somewhat more commendable when unrequited, and art, music, and literature when unappreciated. We give maximal credit when there are quite visible reasons for behaving differently—for example, when the lover is mistreated or the art, music, or literature suppressed.

If we commend a person who puts duty before love, it is because the control exercised by love is easily identified. It has been customary to commend those who live celibate lives, give away their fortunes, or remain loyal to a cause when persecuted, because there are clear reasons for behaving differently. The extent of the credit varies with the magnitude of the opposing conditions. We commend loyalty in proportion to the intensity of the persecution, generosity in proportion to the sacrifices entailed, and celibacy in proportion to a person's inclination to engage in sexual behavior. As La Rochefoucauld observed, "No man deserves to be praised for his goodness unless he has strength of character to be wicked. All other goodness is generally nothing but indolence or impotence of will."

An inverse relation between credit and the conspicuousness of causes is particularly obvious when behavior is explicitly controlled by stimuli. The extent to which we commend someone for operating a complex piece of equipment depends on the circumstances. If it is obvious that he is simply imitating another operator, that someone is "showing him what to do," we give him very little credit—at most only for being able to imitate and execute the behavior. If he is following oral instructions, if someone is "telling him what to do," we give him slightly more credit—at least for understanding the language well enough to follow directions. If he is following written instructions, we give him additional credit for knowing how to read. But we give him credit for "knowing how to operate the equipment" only if he does so without current direction, though he may have learned through imitation or by following oral or written instructions. We give him maximal credit if he has discovered how to operate it without help, since he then owes nothing to any instructor at any time; his behavior has been shaped wholly by the relatively inconspic- uous contingencies arranged by the equipment, and these are now past history.

Similar examples are to be found in verbal behavior. We reinforce people when they behave verbally—we pay them to read to us, to lecture, or to act in movies and plays —but we use credit to reinforce what is said rather than the act of speaking. Suppose someone makes an important statement. We give him minimal credit if he is simply repeating what another speaker has just said. If he is reading from a text, we give him a little more credit, in part for "knowing how to read." If he is "speaking from memory," no current stimulus is in evidence, and we give him credit for "knowing the statement." If it is clear that the obser- vation is original, that no part of it is derived from the verbal behavior of anyone else, we give maximal credit.

We commend a prompt child more than one who must be reminded of his appointments because the reminder is a particularly visible feature of temporal contingencies. We give more credit to a person for "mental" arithmetic than for arithmetic done on paper because the stimuli controlling successive steps are conspicuous on the paper. The theoretical physicist gets more credit than the experimental because the behavior of the latter clearly depends on laboratory practice and observation. We commend those who behave well without supervision more than those who need to be watched, and those who naturally speak a language more than those who must consult gram- matical rules.

We acknowledge this curious relation between credit and the inconspicuousness of controlling con- ditions when we conceal control to avoid losing credit or to claim credit not really due us. The general does his best to maintain his dignity while riding in a jeep over rough terrain, and the flute player continues to play although a fly crawls over his face. We try not to sneeze or laugh on solemn occasions, and after making an embarrassing mistake we try to act as if we had not done so. We submit to pain without flinching, we eat daintily though ravenous, we reach casually for our winnings at cards, and we risk a burn by slowly putting down a hot plate. (Dr. Johnson questioned the value of this: spewing out a mouthful of hot potato, he exclaimed to his astonished companions, "A fool would have swallowed it!") In other words we resist any condition in which we behave in undignified ways.

We attempt to gain credit by disguising or concealing control. The television speaker uses a prompter which is out of sight, and the lecturer glances only surreptitiously at his notes, and both then appear to be speaking either from memory or extemporaneously, when they are in fact—and less commendably—reading. We try to gain credit by inventing less compelling reasons for our conduct. We "save face" by attributing our behavior to less visible or less powerful causes—by behaving, for example, as if we were not under threat. Following Saint Jerome, we make a virtue of necessity, acting as we are forced to act but as if we were not forced. We conceal coercion by doing more than is required: "If anyone forces you to go one mile, go with him two miles." We try to avoid discredit for objectionable behavior by claiming irresistible reasons; as Choderlos de Laclos observed in *Les liaisons dangereuses*, "A woman must have a pretext in giving herself to a man. What better than to appear to be yielding to force?"

We magnify the credit due us by exposing ourselves to conditions which ordinarily generate unworthy be havior while refraining from acting in unworthy ways. We seek out conditions under which behavior has been positively reinforced and then refuse to engage in the behavior; we court temptation, as the saint in the desert maximized the virtues of an austere life by arranging to have beautiful women or delicious food nearby. We continue to punish ourselves, as flagellants do, when we could readily stop, or submit to the fate of the martyr when we could escape.

When we are concerned with the credit to be given to others, we minimize the conspicuousness of the causes of their behavior. We resort to gentle admonition rather than punishment because conditioned reinforcers are less conspicuous than unconditioned, and avoidance more commendable than escape. We give the student a hint rather than tell him the whole answer, which he will get credit for knowing if the hint suffices. We merely suggest or advise rather than give orders. We give permission to those who are going to behave in objectionable ways anyway, like the bishop who, when presiding at a dinner, exclaimed, "Those who must smoke, may." We make it easy for people to save face by accepting their explanations of their conduct, no matter how unlikely. We test commendability by giving people reasons for behaving uncommendably. Chaucer's patient Griselda proved her fidelity to her husband by resisting the prodigious reasons he gave her for being unfaithful.

Giving credit in inverse proportion to the conspicuousness of the causes of behavior may be simply a matter of good husbandry. We make a judicious use of our resources. There is no point in commending a person for doing what he is going to do anyway, and we estimate the chances from the visible evidence. We are particularly likely to commend a person when we know of no other way of getting results, when there are no other reasons why he should behave in other ways. We do not give credit if it will work no change. We do not waste credit on reflexes, because they can be strengthened only with great difficulty, if at all, through operant reinforcement. We do not give credit for what has been done by accident. We also withhold credit if it is going to be supplied by others; for example, we do not commend people for giving alms if they sound trumpets before doing so, since "they have their reward." (A judicious use of resources is often clearer with respect to punishment. We do not waste punishments when they will work no change—when, for example, the behavior was accidental or emitted by a retarded or psychotic person.)

Good husbandry may also explain why we do not commend people who are obviously working simply for commendation. Behavior is to be commended only if it is more than merely commendable. If those who work for commendation are productive in no other way, the commendation is wasted. It may also interfere with the effects of other consequences; the player who works for applause, who "plays to the grandstand," responds less sensitively to the contingencies of the game.

We seem to be interested in judicious use when we call rewards and punishments just or unjust and fair or unfair. We are concerned with what a person "deserves," or, as the dictionary puts it, what he is "rightfully worthy of, or fairly entitled to, or able to claim rightfully by virtue of action done or qualities displayed." Too generous a reward is more than is needed to maintain the behavior. It is particularly unfair when nothing at all has been done to deserve it or when, in fact, what has been done deserves punishment. Too great a punishment is also unjust, especially when nothing has been done to deserve it or when a person has behaved well. Incommensurate consequences may cause trouble; good fortune often reinforces indolence, for example, and bad fortune often punishes industry. (The reinforcers at issue are not necessarily administered by other people. Good or bad luck causes trouble when it is not deserved.)

We try to correct defective contingencies when we say that a man should "appreciate" his good fortune. We mean that he should henceforth act in ways which would be fairly reinforced by what he has already received. We may hold, in fact, that a man *can* appreciate things only if he has worked for them. (The etymology of "appreciate" is significant: to appreciate the behavior of a man is to put a price on it. "Esteem" and "respect" are related terms. We esteem behavior in the sense of estimating the appropriateness of reinforcement. We respect simply by noticing. Thus, we respect a worthy opponent in the sense that we are alert to his strength. A man wins respect by gaining notice, and we have no respect for those who are "beneath our notice." We no doubt particularly notice the things we esteem or appreciate, but in doing so we do not necessarily place a value on them.)

There is something more than good husbandry or the appropriate evaluation of reinforcers in our concern for dignity or worth. We not only praise, commend, approve, or applaud a person, we "admire" him, and the word is close to "marvel at" or "wonder at." We stand in awe of the inexplicable, and it is therefore not surprising that we are likely to admire behavior more as we understand it less. And, of course, what we do not understand we attribute to autonomous man. The early troubadour reciting a long poem must have seemed possessed (and he himself called upon a muse to inspire him), as the actor reciting memorized lines today seems to be possessed by the character he plays. The gods spoke through oracles and through the priests who recited holy script. Ideas appear miraculously in the unconscious thought processes of intuitive mathematicians, who are therefore admired beyond mathematicians who proceed through reasoned steps. The creative genius of artist, composer, or writer is a kind of genie.

We seem to appeal to the miraculous when we admire behavior because we cannot strengthen it in any other way. We may coerce soldiers into risking their lives, or pay them generously for doing so, and we may not admire them in either case, but to induce a man to risk his life when he does not "have to" and when there are no obvious rewards, nothing seems available but admiration. A difference between expressing admiration and giving credit is clear when we admire behavior which admiration will not affect. We may call a scientific achievement, a work of art, a piece of music, or a book admirable but at such a time or in such a way that we cannot affect the scientist, artist, composer, or writer, even though we should give credit and offer other kinds of support if we could. We admire genetic endowment—the physical beauty, skill, or prowess of a race, family, or individual—but not in order to change it. (The admiration may eventually change genetic endowment by changing selective breeding, but on a very different time scale.)

What we may call the struggle for dignity has many features in common with the struggle for freedom. The removal of a positive reinforcer is aversive, and when people are deprived of credit or admiration or the chance to be commended or admired, they respond in appropriate ways. They escape from those who deprive them or attack in order to weaken their effectiveness.

The literature of dignity identifies those who infringe a person's worth, it describes the practices they use, and it suggests measures to be taken. Like the literature of freedom it is not much concerned with simple escape, presumably because instruction is not needed. Instead it concentrates on weakening those who deprive others of credit. The measures are seldom as violent as those recommended by the literature of freedom, probably because loss of credit is in general less aversive than pain or death. They are often in fact merely verbal; we react to those who deprive us of due credit by protesting, opposing, or condemning them and their practices. (What is felt when a person protests is usually called resentment, significantly defined as "the expression of indignant displeasure," but we do not protest *because* we feel resentful. We both protest *and* feel resentful because we have been deprived of the chance to be admired or to receive credit.)

A large part of the literature of dignity is concerned with justice, with the appropriateness of rewards and punishment. Both freedom and dignity are at stake when the appropriateness of a punishment is being considered. Economic practices come into the literature in determining a fair price or a fair wage. The child's first protest, "That's not fair," is usually a matter of the magnitude of a reward or punishment. We are concerned here with that part of the literature of dignity which protests encroachment on personal worth. A person protests (and incidentally feels indignant) when he is unnecessarily jostled, tripped, or pushed around, forced to work with the wrong tools, tricked into behaving foolishly with joke-shop novelties, or forced to behave in demeaning ways, as in a jail or concentration camp. He protests and resents the addition of any unnecessary control. We offend him by offering to pay for services he has performed as a favor, because we imply a lesser generosity or good will on his part. A student protests when we tell him an answer he already knows, because we destroy the credit he would have been given for knowing it. To give a devout person proof of the existence of God is to destroy his claim to pure faith. The mystic resents orthodoxy; antinomianism took the position that to behave well by following rules was not a sign of true goodness. Civic virtue is not easily demonstrated in the presence of the police. To require a citizen to sign a loyalty oath is to destroy some of the loyalty he could otherwise claim, since any subsequent loyal behavior may then be attributed to the oath.

The artist objects to (and resents) being told that he is painting the kind of picture that sells well, or the author that he is writing potboilers, or the legislator that he is supporting a measure to get votes. We are likely to object to (and resent) being told that we are imitating an admired person, or repeating merely what we have heard someone say or have read in books. We oppose (and resent) any suggestion that the aversive consequences in spite of which we are behaving well are not important. Thus, we object to being told that the mountain we are about to climb is not really difficult, that the enemy we are about to attack is not really formidable, that the work we are doing is not really very hard, or, following La Rochefoucauld, that we are behaving well because we do not have the strength of character to behave badly. When P. W. Bridgman argued that scientists are particularly inclined to admit and correct their mistakes because in science a mistake will soon be discovered by someone, he was felt to be challenging the virtue of scientists.

From time to time, advances in physical and biological technology have seemed to threaten worth or dignity when they have reduced chances to earn credit or be admired. Medical science has reduced the need to suffer in silence and the chance to be admired for doing so. Fireproof buildings leave no room for brave firemen, or safe ships for brave sailors, or safe airplanes for brave pilots. The modern dairy barn has no place for a Hercules. When exhausting and dangerous work is no longer required, those who are hard-working and brave seem merely foolish.

The literature of dignity conflicts here with the literature of freedom, which favors a reduction in aversive features of daily life, as by making behavior less arduous, dangerous, or painful, but a concern for personal worth sometimes triumphs over freedom from aversive stimulation—for example, when, quite apart from medical issues, painless childbirth is not as readily accepted as painless dentistry. A military expert, J. F. C. Fuller, has written: "The highest military rewards are given for bravery and not for intelligence, and the introduction of any novel weapon which detracts from individual prowess is met with opposition." Some labor-saving devices are still opposed on the grounds that they reduce the value of the product. Hand sawyers presumably opposed the introduction of sawmills and destroyed them because their jobs were threatened, but it is also significant that the mills reduced the value of their labor by reducing the value of sawed planks. In this conflict, however, freedom usually wins out over dignity. People have been admired for submitting to danger, hard labor, and pain, but almost everyone is willing to forgo the acclaim for doing so.

Behavioral technology does not escape as easily as physical and biological technology because it threatens too many occult qualities. The alphabet was a great invention, which enabled men to store and transmit records of their verbal behavior and to learn with little effort what others had learned the hard way—that is, to learn from books rather than from direct, possibly painful, contact with the real world. But until men understood the extraordinary advantages of being able to learn from the experience of others, the apparent destruction of personal merit was objectionable. In Plato's *Phaedrus*, Thamus, the Egyptian king, protests that those who learn from books have only the show of wisdom, not wisdom itself. Merely reading what some-one has written is less commendable than saying the same thing for arcane reasons. A person who reads a book appears to be omniscient, yet, according to Thamus, he "knows nothing." And when a text is used to aid memory, Thamus contended that memory would fall into disuse. To read is less commendable than to recite what one has learned. And there are many other ways in which, by reducing the need for exhausting, painful, and dangerous work, a behavioral technology reduces the chance to be admired. The slide rule, the calculating machine, and the computer are the enemies of the arithmetic mind. But here again the gain in freedom from aversive stimulation may compensate for any loss of admiration.

There may seem to be no compensating gain when dignity or worth seems lessened by a basic scientific analysis, apart from technological applications. It is in the nature of scientific progress that the functions of autonomous man be taken over one by one as the role of the environment is better understood. A scientific conception seems demeaning because nothing is even-tually left for which autonomous man can take credit And as for admiration in the sense of wonderment, the behavior we admire is the behavior we cannot yet ex-plain. Science naturally seeks a fuller explanation of that behavior; its goal is the destruction of mystery. The defenders of dignity will protest, but in doing so they postpone an achievement for which, in traditional terms, man would receive the greatest credit and for which he would be most admired.

* * *

We recognize a person's dignity or worth when we give him credit for what he has done. The amount we give is inversely proportional to the conspicuousness of the causes of his behavior. If we do not know why a person acts as he does, we attribute his behavior to him. We try to gain additional credit for ourselves by concealing the reasons why we behave in given ways or by claiming to have acted for less powerful reasons. We avoid infringing on the credit due to others by controlling them inconspicuously. We admire people to the extent that we cannot explain what they do, and the word "admire" then means "marvel at." What we may call the literature of dignity is concerned with preserving due credit. It may oppose advances in technology, including a technology of behavior, because they destroy chances to be admired and a basic analysis because it offers an alternative explanation of behavior for which the individual himself has previously been given credit. The literature thus stands in the way of further human achievements.

4
Punishment

FREEDOM IS SOMETIMES DEFINED as a lack of resistance or restraint. A wheel turns freely if there is very little friction in the bearing, a horse breaks free from the post to which it has been tethered, a man frees himself from the branch on which he has been caught while climbing a tree. Physical restraint is an obvious condition, which seems particularly useful in defining freedom, but with respect to important issues, it is a metaphor and not a very good one. People are indeed controlled by fetters, handcuffs, strait jackets, and the walls of jails and concentration camps, but what may be called behavioral control—the restraint imposed by contingencies of reinforcement—is a very different thing.

Except when physically restrained, a person is least free or dignified when he is under threat of punishment, and unfortunately most people often are. Punishment is very common in nature, and we learn a great deal from it. A child runs awkwardly, falls, and is hurt; he touches a bee and is stung; he takes a bone from a dog and is bitten; and as a result he learns not to do these things again. It is mainly to avoid various forms of natural punishment that people have built a more comfortable and less dangerous world.

The word punishment is usually confined to contingencies intentionally arranged by other people, who arrange them because the results are reinforcing to them. (Punitive contingencies are not to be confused with aversive control, through which people are induced to behave in given ways. Punishment is used to induce people *not* to behave in given ways.) A person resorts to punishment when he criticizes, ridicules, blames, or physically attacks another in order to suppress unwanted behavior. Government is often defined in terms of the power to punish, and some religions teach that sinful behavior will be followed by eternal punishments of the most horrible sort.

We should expect the literatures of freedom and dignity to oppose measures of this sort and to work toward a world in which punishment is less common or even absent, and up to a point they have done so. But punitive sanctions are still common. People still control each other more often through censure or blame than commendation or praise, the military and the police remain the most powerful arms of government, communicants are still occasionally reminded of hellfire, and teachers have abandoned the birch rod only to replace it with more subtle forms of punishment. And the curious fact is that those who defend freedom and dignity are not only not opposed to these measures but largely responsible for the fact that they are still with us. This strange state of affairs can be understood only by looking at the way in which organisms respond to punitive contingencies.

Punishment is designed to remove awkward, dangerous, or otherwise unwanted behavior from a repertoire on the assumption that a person who has been punished is less likely to behave in the same way again. Unfortunately, the matter is not that simple. Reward and punishment do not differ merely in the direction of the changes they induce. A child who has been severely punished for sex play is not necessarily less inclined to continue; and a man who has been imprisoned for violent assault is not necessarily less inclined toward violence. Punished behavior is likely to reappear after the punitive contingencies are withdrawn.

What seem to be the intended effects of punishment can often be explained in other ways. For example, punishment may generate incompatible emotions. A boy who has been severely punished for sex play may no longer be, as we might say, in the mood to continue, and fleeing to escape from a punisher is incompatible with attacking him. Future occasions for sex play or for violent assault may evoke similar incompatible behavior through conditioning. Whether the effect is felt as shame, guilt, or a sense of sin depends upon whether the punishment is administered by parent or peer, by a government, or by a church, respectively.

The aversive condition brought about by punishment (and felt in these different ways) has a much more important effect. Quite literally, a person may subsequently behave "in order to avoid punishment." He can avoid it by not behaving in punishable ways, but there are other possibilities. Some of these are disruptive and maladaptive or neurotic, and as a result they have been closely studied. The so-called "dynamisms" of Freud are said to be ways in which repressed wishes evade the censor and find expression, but they can be interpreted simply as ways in which people avoid punishment. Thus, a person may behave in ways that will not be punished because they cannot be seen, as by *fantasying* or *dreaming*. He may *sublimate* by engaging in behavior which has rather similar reinforcing effects but is not punished. He may *displace* punishable behavior by directing it toward objects which cannot punish—for example, he may be aggressive toward physical objects, children, or small animals. He may watch or read about others who engage in punishable behavior, *identifying* himself with them, or interpret the behavior of others as punishable, *projecting* his own tendencies. He may *rationalize* his behavior by giving reasons, either to himself or others, which make it nonpunishable—as in asserting that he is punishing a child for the child's own good.

There are more effective ways of avoiding punishment. One may avoid occasions on which punishable behavior is likely to occur. A person who has been punished for drunkenness may "put temptation behind him" by staying away from places where he is likely to drink too much; a student who has been punished for not studying may avoid situations in which he is distracted from his work. Still another strategy is to change the environment so that behavior is less likely to be punished. We reduce natural punishing contingencies when we repair a broken stairway so that we are less likely to fall, and we weaken punitive social contingencies by associating with more tolerant friends.

Still another strategy is to change the probability that punishable behavior will occur. A person who is frequently punished because he is quick to anger may count to ten before acting; he avoids punishment if, while he is counting, his inclination to act aggressively drops to a manageable level. Or he may make punishable behavior less likely by changing his physiological condition, controlling aggression, for example, by taking a tranquilizer. Men have even resorted to surgical means—castrating themselves, for example, or following the Biblical injunction to cut off the hand that offends. Punitive contingencies may also induce a man to seek out or construct environments in which he is likely to engage in behavior which displaces punishable forms; he stays out of trouble by keeping busy in

nonpunished ways, as by doggedly "doing something
else." (Much behavior which appears irrational in the
sense that it seems to have no positively reinforcing
consequences may have the effect of displacing behavior which is subject to punishment.) A person may
even take steps to strengthen contingencies which teach
him to stop behaving in punishable ways: he may, for
example, take drugs under the influence of which
smoking or drinking has strong aversive consequences,
such as nausea, or he may expose himself to stronger
ethical, religious, or governmental sanctions.

All these things a person may do to reduce the chances
that he will be punished, but they may also be done
for him by other people. Physical technology has reduced the number of occasions upon which people are
naturally punished, and social environments have been
changed to reduce the likelihood of punishment at the
hands of others. Some familiar strategies may be noted.
 Punishable behavior can be minimized by creating
circumstances in which it is not likely to occur. The
archetypal pattern is the cloister. In a world in which
only simple foods are available, and in moderate supply, no one is subject to the natural punishment of
overeating, or the social punishment of disapproval, or
the religious punishment of gluttony as a venial sin.
Heterosexual behavior is impossible when the sexes are
segregated, and the vicarious sexual behavior evoked
by pornography is impossible in the absence of pornographic material. "Prohibition" was an effort to control the consumption of alcohol by removing alcohol
from the environment. It is still practiced in some states
and almost universally to the extent that alcohol cannot
be sold to minors or to anyone at certain times of day
or on certain days. The care of the institutionalized
alcoholic usually involves the control of supplies. The

use of other addictive drugs is still controlled in the same way. Aggressive behavior which is otherwise uncontrollable is suppressed by putting a person in solitary confinement, where there is no one to aggress against. Theft is controlled by locking up everything likely to be stolen.

Another possibility is to break up the contingencies under which punished behavior is reinforced. Temper tantrums often disappear when they no longer receive attention, aggressive behavior is attenuated by making sure that nothing is gained by it, and overeating is controlled by making foods less palatable. Another technique is to arrange circumstances under which behavior may occur without being punished. Saint Paul recommended marriage as a means of reducing objectionable forms of sexual behavior, and pornography has been recommended for the same reasons. Literature and art permit one to "sublimate" other kinds of troublesome behavior. Punishable behavior can also be suppressed by strongly reinforcing any behavior which displaces it. Organized sports are sometimes promoted on the grounds that they provide an environment in which young people will be too busy to get into trouble. If all this fails, punishable behavior may be made less likely by changing physiological conditions. Hormones may be used to change sexual behavior, surgery (as in lobotomy) to control violence, tranquilizers to control aggression, and appetite depressants to control overeating.

Measures of this sort are no doubt often inconsistent with each other and may have unforeseen consequences. It proved to be impossible to control the supply of alcohol during prohibition, and segregation of the sexes may lead to unwanted homosexuality. Excessive suppression of behavior which would otherwise be strongly reinforced may lead to defection from the punishing

group. These problems are in essence soluble, however, and it should be possible to design a world in
which behavior likely to be punished seldom or never
occurs. We try to design such a world for those who
cannot solve the problem of punishment for themselves, such as babies, retardates, or psychotics, and
if it could be done for everyone, much time and energy
would be saved.

The defenders of freedom and dignity object to solving
the problem of punishment that way. Such a world
builds only automatic goodness. T. H. Huxley saw
nothing wrong with it: "If some great power would
agree to make me always think what is true and do
what is right, on condition of being some sort of a
clock and wound up every morning before I got out of
bed, I should close instantly with the offer." But Joseph
Wood Krutch refers to this as the scarcely believable
position of a "proto-modern," and he shares T. S. Eliot's
contempt for "systems so perfect that no one will need
to be good."

The trouble is that when we punish a person for behaving badly, we leave it up to him to discover how to
behave well, and he can then get credit for behaving
well. But if he behaves well for the reasons we have
just examined, it is the environment that must get the
credit. At issue is an attribute of autonomous man.
Men are to behave well only because they are good.
Under a "perfect" system no one needs goodness.

There are, of course, valid reasons for thinking less
of a person who is only automatically good, for he is a
lesser person. In a world in which he does not need to
work hard, he will not learn to sustain hard work. In a
world in which medical science has alleviated pain, he
will not learn to take painful stimuli. In a world which
promotes automatic goodness, he will not learn to take

the punishments associated with behaving badly. To prepare people for a world in which they cannot be good automatically, we need appropriate instruction, but that does not mean a permanently punitive environment, and there is no reason why progress toward a world in which people may be automatically good should be impeded. The problem is to induce people not to be good but to behave well.

The issue is again the visibility of control. As environmental contingencies become harder to see, the goodness of autonomous man becomes more apparent, and there are several reasons why punitive control becomes inconspicuous. A simple way to avoid punishment is to avoid punishers. Sex play becomes surreptitious, and a violent man attacks only when the police are not around. But the punisher may offset this by concealment. Parents frequently spy on their children, and policemen wear plain clothes. Escape must then become more subtle. If motorists obey speed laws only when the police are visible, speed may be monitored by radar, but the motorist may then install an electronic device which tells him when radar is in use. A state which converts all its citizens into spies or a religion which promotes the concept of an all-seeing God makes escape from the punisher practically impossible, and punitive contingencies are then maximally effective. People behave well although there is no visible supervision.

But the absence of a supervisor is easily misunderstood. It is commonly said that the control becomes internalized, which is simply another way of saying that it passes from the environment to autonomous man, but what happens is that it becomes less visible. One kind of control said to be internalized is represented by the Judaeo-Christian conscience and the Freudian superego. These indwelling agents speak in a still, small voice, telling a person what to do and, in particular, what not to do. The words are acquired from the community. The conscience and the superego are the vicars of society, and theologians and psychoanalysts alike recognize their external origins. Where the Old Adam or the id speaks for the personal good specified by man's genetic endowment, the conscience or superego speaks for what is good for others.

The conscience or superego does not arise simply from the concealment of punishers. It represents a number of auxiliary practices which make punitive sanctions more effective. We help a person avoid punishment by telling him about punitive contingencies, we warn him not to behave in ways which are likely to be punished, and we advise him to behave in ways which will not be punished. Many religious and governmental laws have these effects. They describe the contingencies under which some forms of behavior are punished and others not. Maxims, proverbs, and other forms of folk wisdom often supply useful rules. "Look before you leap" is an injunction derived from an analysis of certain kinds of contingencies: leaping without looking is more likely to be punished than looking and then possibly not leaping or leaping more skillfully. "Do not steal" is an injunction derived from social contingencies: people punish thieves.

By following the rules which others have derived from punitive contingencies in the natural and social environment a person can often avoid or escape punishment. Both the rules and the contingencies which generate rule-following behavior may be conspicuous, but they may also be learned and later remembered, and the process then becomes invisible. The individual tells himself what to do and what not to do, and it is easy to lose sight of the fact that he has been taught to do so by the verbal community. When a person derives his own rules from an analysis of punitive contingencies, we are particularly likely to give him credit for the good behavior which follows, but the visible stages have simply faded farther into history.

When the punitive contingencies are simply part of the nonsocial environment, it is reasonably clear what is happening. We do not allow a person to learn to drive a car by exposing him to serious punitive contingencies. We do not send him onto a busy highway without preparation and hold him responsible for everything that happens. We give him instruction in safe and skillful driving. We teach him rules. We let him begin to drive in a training device in which punitive contingencies are minimized or altogether lacking. We then take him onto a relatively safe highway. If we are successful, we may produce a safe and skillful driver without resorting to punishment at all, even though the contingencies under which he will drive for the rest of his life continue to be highly punitive. We are likely to say, without warrant, that he has acquired the "knowledge" he needs in order to drive safely or that he is now a "good driver" rather than a person who drives well. When the contingencies are social, and in particular when they are arranged by religious agencies, we are much more likely to infer an "inner knowledge of right" or an inner goodness.

The goodness to which good behavior is attributed is part of a person's worth or dignity and shows the same inverse relationship to the visibility of control. We attribute the greatest goodness to people who have never behaved badly and hence have never been punished and who behave well without following rules. Jesus is usually portrayed as such a person. We infer a lesser goodness in those who behave well but only because they have been punished. The reformed sinner may resemble a natural saint, but the fact that

he has been exposed to punitive contingencies places
some limit on his natural goodness. Close to the reformed sinner are those who have analyzed the punitive contingencies in their environments and derived
rules which they have followed to avoid punishment.
A lesser amount of goodness is attributed to those who
follow rules formulated by others, and very little if
the rules and the contingencies which maintain rule-
governed behavior are conspicuous. We attribute no
goodness at all to those who behave well only under
constant supervision by a punitive agent such as the
police.

Goodness, like other aspects of dignity or worth,
waxes as visible control wanes, and so, of course, does
freedom. Hence goodness and freedom tend to be
associated. John Stuart Mill held that the only goodness worthy of the name was displayed by a person
who behaved well although it was possible for him to
behave badly and that only such a person was free.
Mill was not in favor of closing houses of prostitution;
they were to remain open so that people could achieve
freedom and dignity through self-control. But the argument is convincing only if we neglect the reasons why
people behave well when it is apparently possible for
them to behave badly. It is one thing to prohibit the
use of dice and playing cards, to prohibit the sale of
alcohol, and to close houses of prostitution. It is another thing to make all these things aversive, as by
punishing the behavior they evoke, by calling them
temptations contrived by the devil, and by portraying
the tragic fate of the drunkard or describing the vene-
real diseases acquired from prostitutes. The effect may
be the same: people may not gamble, drink, or go to
prostitutes, but the fact that they *cannot* do so in one
environment and *do not* do so in the other is a fact
about techniques of control, not about goodness or

freedom. In one environment the reasons for behaving well are clear; in another they are easily overlooked and forgotten.

It is sometimes said that children are not ready for the freedom of self-control until they reach the age of reason, and that meanwhile they must either be kept in a safe environment or be punished. If punishment may be postponed until they reach the age of reason, it may be dispensed with altogether. But this means simply that safe environments and punishment are the only measures available until a child has been exposed to the contingencies which give him other reasons for behaving well. Appropriate contingencies can often not be arranged for primitive people, and the same confusion between visibility and internalized control is shown when it is said that primitive peoples are not ready for freedom. What, if anything, they are not ready for is a type of control which requires a special history of contingencies.

Many of the issues of punitive control are raised by the concept of responsibility, an attribute which is said to distinguish man from the other animals. The responsible person is a "deserving" person. We give him credit when he behaves well, in order that he will continue to do so, but we are most likely to use the term when what he deserves is punishment. We *hold* a person responsible for his conduct in the sense that he can be justly or fairly punished. This is again a matter of good husbandry, of a judicious use of reinforcers, of "making the punishment fit the crime." More punishment than necessary is costly and may suppress desirable behavior, while too little is wasteful if it has no effect at all.

The legal determination of responsibility (and justice) is in part concerned with facts. Did a person,

indeed, behave in a given way? Were the circumstances such that the behavior was punishable under
the law? If so, what laws apply, and what punishments
are specified? But other questions seem to concern the
inner man. Was the act intentional or premeditated?
Was it done in the heat of anger? Did the person know
the difference between right and wrong? Was he
aware of the possible consequences of his act? All
these questions about purposes, feelings, knowledge,
and so on, can be restated in terms of the environment
to which a person has been exposed. What a person
"intends to do" depends upon what he has done in the
past and what has then happened. A person does not
act because he "feels angry"; he acts *and* feels angry
for a common reason, not specified. Whether he deserves punishment when all these conditions are taken
into account is a question about probable results: will
he, if punished, behave in a different way when similar
circumstances again arise? There is a current tendency
to substitute controllability for responsibility, and controllability is not so likely to be regarded as a possession of autonomous man, since it explicitly alludes to
external conditions.

The assertion that "only a free man can be responsible for his conduct" has two meanings, depending
upon whether we are interested in freedom or responsibility. If we want to say that people are responsible,
we must do nothing to infringe their freedom, since
if they are not free to act they cannot be held responsible. If we want to say they are free, we must hold
them responsible for their behavior by maintaining
punitive contingencies, since if they behaved in the
same way under conspicuous nonpunitive contingencies, it would be clear that they were not free.

Any move toward an environment in which men are
automatically good threatens responsibility. In the

control of alcoholism, for example, the traditional practice is punitive. Drunkenness is called wrong, and ethical sanctions are imposed by a person's peers (the condition generated being felt as shame), or it is classified as illegal and subject to governmental sanctions (the condition generated being felt as guilt), or it is called sinful and punished by religious agencies (the condition generated being felt as a sense of sin). The practice has not been conspicuously successful, and other controlling measures have been sought. Certain medical evidence appears to be relevant. People differ in their tolerances to alcohol and their addictive dependencies. Once a person has become an alcoholic, he may drink to relieve severe withdrawal symptoms which are not always taken into account by those who have never experienced them. The medical aspects raise the question of responsibility: how fair is it to punish the alcoholic? From the point of view of husbandry, can we expect punishment to be effective against the opposing positive contingencies? Should we not rather treat the medical condition? (Our culture differs from the Erewhon of Samuel Butler in imposing no punitive sanctions on illness.) As responsibility diminishes, punishment is relaxed.

Juvenile delinquency is another example. In the traditional view a young person is responsible for obeying the law and may be justly punished if he disobeys, but effective punitive contingencies are hard to maintain, and other measures have therefore been sought. Evidence that delinquency is commoner in certain kinds of neighborhoods and among poorer people seems relevant. A person is more likely to steal if he has little or nothing of his own, if his education has not prepared him to get and hold a job so that he may buy what he needs, if no jobs are available, if he has not been taught to obey the law, or if he often sees others breaking the law with impunity. Under such conditions delinquent behavior is powerfully reinforced and unlikely to be suppressed by legal sanctions. Contingencies are therefore relaxed: the delinquent may simply be warned or his sentence suspended. Responsibility and punishment decline together.

The real issue is the effectiveness of techniques of control. We shall not solve the problems of alcoholism and juvenile delinquency by increasing a sense of responsibility. It is the environment which is "responsible" for the objectional behavior, and it is the environment, not some attribute of the individual, which must be changed. We recognize this when we talk about the punitive contingencies in the natural environment. Running head-on into a wall is punished by a blow to the skull, but we do not hold a man responsible for not running into walls nor do we say that nature holds him responsible. Nature simply punishes him when he runs into a wall. When we make the world less punishing or teach people how to avoid natural punishments, as by giving them rules to follow, we are not destroying responsibility or threatening any other occult quality. We are simply making the world safer.

The concept of responsibility is particularly weak when behavior is traced to genetic determiners. We may admire beauty, grace, and sensitivity, but we do not blame a person because he is ugly, spastic, or color blind. Less conspicuous forms of genetic endowment nevertheless cause trouble. Individuals presumably differ, as species differ, in the extent to which they respond aggressively or are reinforced when they effect aggressive damage, or in the extent to which they engage in sexual behavior or are affected by sexual reinforcement. Are they, therefore, equally responsible for controlling their aggressive or sexual behavior, and

is it fair to punish them to the same extent? If we do
not punish a person for a club foot, should we punish
him for being quick to anger or highly susceptible to
sexual reinforcement? The issue has recently been
raised by the possibility that many criminals show an
anomaly in their chromosomes. The concept of responsibility offers little help. The issue is controllability.
We cannot change genetic defects by punishment; we
can work only through genetic measures which operate
on a much longer time scale. What must be changed
is not the responsibility of autonomous man but the
conditions, environmental or genetic, of which a person's behavior is a function.

Although people object when a scientific analysis traces
their behavior to external conditions and thus deprives
them of credit and the chance to be admired, they
seldom object when the same analysis absolves them
of blame. The crude environmentalism of the eighteenth
and nineteenth centuries was quickly put to use for
purposes of exoneration and exculpation. George Eliot
ridiculed it. The rector in *Adam Bede* exclaims, "Why,
yes, a man can't very well steal a bank-note unless the
bank-note lies within convenient reach; but he won't
make us think him an honest man because he begins
to howl at the bank-note for falling in his way." The
alcoholic is the first to claim that he is ill, and the
juvenile delinquent that he is the victim of an unfavor-
able background; if they are not responsible, they cannot be justly punished.

Exoneration is in a sense the obverse of responsibility. Those who undertake to do something about human
behavior—for any reason whatsoever—become part of
the environment to which responsibility shifts. In the
old view it was the student who failed, the child who
went wrong, the citizen who broke the law, and the

poor who were poor because they were idle, but it is
now commonly said that there are no dull students but
only poor teachers, no bad children but only bad parents, no delinquency except on the part of law enforcement agencies, and no indolent men but only poor
incentive systems. But of course we must ask in turn
why teachers, parents, governors, and enterpreneurs
are bad. The mistake, as we shall see later, is to put
the responsibility anywhere, to suppose that some-
where a causal sequence is initiated.

Communist Russia provided an interesting case history in the relation between environmentalism and
personal responsibility, as Raymond Bauer has pointed
out. Immediately after the revolution the government
could argue that if many Russians were uneducated,
unproductive, badly behaved, and unhappy, it was
because their environment had made them so. The new
government would change the environment, making
use of Pavlov's work on conditioned reflexes, and all
would be well. But by the early thirties the government
had had its chance, and many Russians were still not
conspicuously better informed, more productive, better
behaved, or happier. The official line was then changed,
and Pavlov went out of favor. A strongly purposive
psychology was substituted: it was up to the Russian
citizen to get an education, work productively, behave
well, and be happy. The Russian educator was to make
sure that he would accept this responsibility, but not
by conditioning him. The successes of the Second
World War restored confidence in the earlier principle,
however; the government had been successful after all.
It might not yet be completely effective, but it was
moving in the right direction. Pavlov came back into
favor.

Exoneration of the controller is seldom so easily
documented, but something of the sort probably always

underlies the continued use of punitive methods. Attacks on automatic goodness may show a concern for autonomous man, but the practical contingencies are more cogent. The literatures of freedom and dignity have made the control of human behavior a punishable offense, largely by holding the controller responsible for aversive results. The controller can escape responsibility if he can maintain the position that the individual himself is in control. The teacher who gives the student credit for learning can also blame him for not learning. The parent who gives his child credit for his achievements can also blame him for his mistakes. Neither the teacher nor the parent can be held responsible.

The genetic sources of human behavior are particularly useful in exoneration. If some races are less intelligent than others, the teacher cannot be blamed if he does not teach them as well. If some men are born criminals, the law will always be broken no matter how perfect the enforcing agency. If men make war because they are by nature aggressive, we need not be ashamed of our failure to keep the peace. A concern for exoneration is indicated by the fact that we are more likely to appeal to genetic endowment to explain undesirable results than positive accomplishments. Those who are currently interested in doing something about human behavior cannot be given credit for, or blamed for, consequences which can be traced to genetic sources; if they have any responsibility, it is to the future of the species. The practice of attributing behavior to genetic endowment—of the species as a whole or of some subdivision like a race or family—may affect breeding practices and eventually other ways of changing that endowment, and the contemporary individual may in a sense be held responsible for the consequences if he acts or fails to act, but the consequences are remote and raise a different kind of problem, to which we shall eventually turn.

Those who use punishment seem always to be on the safe side. Everyone approves the suppression of wrongdoing, except the wrongdoer. If those who are punished do not then do right, it is not the punisher's fault. But the exoneration is not complete. Even those who do right may take a long time to discover what to do and may never do it well. They spend time fumbling with irrelevant facts and wrestling with the devil, and in unnecessary trial-and-error exploration. Moreover, punishment causes pain, and no one wholly escapes or remains untouched even when the pain is suffered by others. The punisher cannot therefore entirely escape criticism, and he may "justify" his action by pointing to consequences of punishment which offset its aversive features.

It would be absurd to include the writings of Joseph de Maistre in the literatures of freedom and dignity, for he was bitterly opposed to their cardinal principles, particularly as expressed by the writers of the Enlightenment. Nevertheless, by opposing effective alternatives to punishment on the ground that punishment alone leaves the individual free to choose to behave well, those literatures have created a need for a kind of justification of which de Maistre was a master. Here is his defense of perhaps the most horrible of all punishers—the torturer and executioner.

A somber signal is given: an abject minister of justice comes to knock at his door and let him know that he is needed. He sets out; he arrives at the public square, which is crowded with an eager excited throng. A prisoner or a murderer or a blasphemer is given over to him. He seizes him and stretches and ties him on a horizontal cross; he lifts his arm and a horrible silence falls. Nothing is heard but the cry of the bones cracking under the heavy rod and the howlings of the victim. Then he unties him and carries him to the wheel; the shattered limbs get twisted in the spokes; the head hangs; the hair stands out; and from the mouth, gaping open like a stove, come only now a few bloody words which at intervals beg for death. Now the executioner has finished; his heart beats, but it is for joy; he applauds himself, he says in his heart: "Nobody is better at the wheel than I!" He comes down and holds out his blood-stained hand, and the Law throws into it from a distance some gold pieces which he carries away with him through a double hedge of people who draw away in horror. He sits down to table and eats; then he gets into bed and goes to sleep. When he wakes up the next day, he begins to think about something quite different from the work he has been doing the day before. . . . All grandeur, all power, all discipline are founded on the executioner. He is the horror of the human association and the tie that holds it together. Take out of the world this incomprehensible agent, and at that instant will order give way to chaos, thrones fall and society vanish. God, who is the source of all sovereignty, is, therefore, the source of punishment, too.

If we no longer resort to torture in what we call the civilized world, we nevertheless still make extensive use of punitive techniques in both domestic and foreign relations. And apparently for good reasons. Nature if not God has created man in such a way that he can be controlled punitively. People quickly become skillful punishers (if not, thereby, skillful controllers), whereas alternative positive measures are not easily learned. The need for punishment seems to have the support of history, and alternative practices threaten the cherished values of freedom and dignity. And so we go on punishing—and defending punishment. A contemporary de Maistre might defend war in similar terms: "All grandeur, all power, all discipline are founded on the soldier. He is the horror of the human association and the tie that holds it together. Take out of the world this incomprehensible agent, and at that instant will order give way to chaos, governments fall and society vanish. God, who is the source of all sovereignty, is, therefore, the source of war, too."

Yet there are better ways, and the literatures of freedom and dignity are not pointing to them.

* * *

Except when physically constrained, a person is least free or dignified when under the threat of punishment. We should expect that the literatures of freedom and dignity would oppose punitive techniques, but in fact they have acted to preserve them. A person who has been punished is not thereby simply less inclined to behave in a given way; at best, he learns how to avoid punishment. Some ways of doing so are maladaptive or neurotic, as in the so-called "Freudian dynamisms." Other ways include avoiding situations in which punished behavior is likely to occur and doing things which are incompatible with punished behavior. Other people may take similar steps to reduce the likelihood that a person will be punished, but the literatures of freedom and dignity object to this as leading only to automatic goodness. Under punitive contingencies a person appears to be free to behave well and to deserve credit when he does so. Nonpunitive contingencies generate the same behavior, but a person cannot then be said to be free, and the contingencies deserve the credit when he behaves well. Little or nothing remains for autonomous man to do and receive credit for doing. He does not engage in moral struggle and therefore has no chance to be a moral hero or credited with inner virtues. But our task is not to encourage moral struggle or to build or demonstrate inner virtues. It is to make life less punishing and in doing so to release for more reinforcing activities the time and energy consumed in the avoidance of punishment. Up to a point the literatures of freedom and dignity have played a part in the slow and erratic alleviation of aversive features of the human environment, including the aversive features used in intentional control. But they have formulated the task in such a way that they cannot now accept the fact that all control is exerted by the environment and proceed to the design of better environments rather than of better men.

5
Alternatives to Punishment

THOSE WHO CHAMPION FREEDOM AND DIG-
nity do not, of course, confine themselves to punitive
measures, but they turn to alternatives with diffidence
and timidity. Their concern for autonomous man com-
mits them to only ineffective measures, several of which
we may now examine.

PERMISSIVENESS

An all-out permissiveness has been seriously advanced as an alternative to punishment. No control at
all is to be exerted, and the autonomy of the individual
will therefore remain unchallenged. If a person behaves well, it is because he is either innately good or
self-controlled. Freedom and dignity are guaranteed.
A free and virtuous man needs no government (governments only corrupt), and under anarchy he can be
naturally good and admired for being so. He needs no
orthodox religion; he is pious, and he behaves piously
without following rules, perhaps with the help of direct
mystical experience. He needs no organized economic
incentives; he is naturally industrious and will exchange part of what he owns with others on fair terms
under the natural conditions of supply and demand.
He needs no teacher; he learns because he loves learning, and his natural curiosity dictates what he needs

to know. If life becomes too complex or if his natural status is disturbed by accidents or the intrusion of would-be controllers, he may have personal problems, but he will find his own solutions without the direction of a psychotherapist.

Permissive practices have many advantages. They save the labor of supervision and the enforcement of sanctions. They do not generate counterattack. They do not expose the practitioner to the charge of restricting freedom or destroying dignity. They exonerate him when things go wrong. If men behave badly toward each other in a permissive world, it is because human nature is less than perfect. If they fight when there is no government to preserve order, it is because they have aggressive instincts. If a child becomes delinquent when his parents have made no effort to control him, it is because he has associated with the wrong people or has criminal tendencies.

Permissiveness is not, however, a policy; it is the abandonment of policy, and its apparent advantages are illusory. To refuse to control is to leave control not to the person himself, but to other parts of the social and nonsocial environments.

THE CONTROLLER AS MIDWIFE

A method of modifying behavior without appearing to exert control is represented by Socrates' metaphor of the midwife: one person helps another give birth to behavior. Since the midwife plays no part in conception and only a small part in parturition, the person who gives birth to the behavior may take full credit for it. Socrates demonstrated the art of midwifery, or maieutics, in education. He pretended to show how an

uneducated slave boy could be led to prove Pythagoras'
theorem for doubling the square. The boy assented to
the steps in the proof, and Socrates claimed that he did
so without being told—in other words, that he "knew"
the theorem in some sense all along. Socrates contended that even ordinary knowledge could be drawn
out in the same way since the soul knew the truth and
needed only to be shown that it knew it. The episode
is often cited as if it were relevant to modern educational practice.

The metaphor appears also in theories of psychotherapy. The patient is not to be told how to behave
more effectively or given directions for solving his
problems; a solution is already within him and has
only to be drawn out with the help of the midwife-
therapist. As one writer has put it: "Freud shared with
Socrates three principles: know thyself; virtue is knowledge; and the maieutic method, or the art of midwifery, which is, of course, the [psycho-] analytic
process." Similar practices in religion are associated
with mysticism: a person does not need to follow
rules, as orthodoxy would have it; right behavior will
well up from inner sources.

Intellectual, therapeutic, and moral midwifery is
scarcely easier than punitive control, because it demands rather subtle skills and concentrated attention,
but it has its advantages. It seems to confer a strange
power on the practitioner. Like the cabalistic use of
hints and allusions, it achieves results seemingly out of
proportion to the measures employed. The apparent
contribution of the individual is not reduced, however.
He is given full credit for knowing before he learns,
for having within him the seeds of good mental health,
and for being able to enter into direct communication
with God. An important advantage is that the prac-

titioner avoids responsibility. Just as it is not the midwife's fault if the baby is stillborn or deformed, so the
teacher is exonerated when the student fails, the psychotherapist when the patient does not solve his problem, and the mystical religious leader when his disciples
behave badly.

Maieutic practices have their place. Just how much
help the teacher should give the student as he acquires
new forms of behavior is a delicate question. The
teacher should wait for the student to respond rather
than rush to tell him what he is to do or say. As
Comenius put it, the more the teacher teaches, the less
the student learns. The student gains in other ways.
In general, we do not like to be told either what we
already know or what we are unlikely ever to know
well or to good effect. We do not read books if we are
already thoroughly familiar with the material or if it is
so completely unfamiliar that it is likely to remain so.
We read books which help us say things we are on the
verge of saying anyway but cannot quite say without
help. We understand the author, although we could
not have formulated what we understand before he
put it into words. There are similar advantages for the
patient in psychotherapy. Maieutic practices are helpful, too, because they exert more control than is usually
acknowledged and some of it may be valuable.

These advantages, however, are far short of the
claims made. Socrates' slave boy learned nothing; there
was no evidence whatever that he could have gone
through the theorem by himself afterward. And it is as
true of maieutics as of permissiveness that positive
results must be credited to unacknowledged controls
of other sorts. If the patient finds a solution without
the help of his therapist, it is because he has been
exposed to a helpful environment elsewhere.

GUIDANCE

Another metaphor associated with weak practices is horticultural. The behavior to which a person has given birth grows, and it may be guided or trained, as a growing plant is trained. Behavior may be "cultivated."

The metaphor is particularly at home in education. A school for small children is a child-garden, or kindergarten. The behavior of the child "develops" until he reaches "maturity." A teacher may accelerate the process or turn it in slightly different directions, but—in the classical phrase—he cannot teach, he can only help the student learn. The metaphor of guidance is also common in psychotherapy. Freud argued that a person must pass through several developmental stages, and that if the patient has become "fixated" at a given stage, the therapist must help him break loose and move forward. Governments engage in guidance—for example, when they encourage the "development" of industry through tax exemptions or provide a "climate" that is favorable to the improvement of race relations.

Guidance is not as easy as permissiveness, but it is usually easier than midwifery, and it has some of the same advantages. One who merely guides a natural development cannot easily be accused of trying to control it. Growth remains an achievement of the individual, testifying to his freedom and worth, his "hidden propensities," and as the gardener is not responsible for the ultimate form of what he grows, so one who merely guides is exonerated when things go wrong.

Guidance is effective, however, only to the extent that control is exerted. To guide is either to open new opportunities or to block growth in particular directions. To arrange an opportunity is not a very positive act, but it is nevertheless a form of control if it increases the likelihood that behavior will be emitted. The teacher who merely selects the material the student is to study or the therapist who merely suggests a different job or change of scene has exerted control, though it may be hard to detect.

Control is more obvious when growth or development is *prevented*. Censorship blocks access to material needed for development in a given direction; it closes opportunities. De Tocqueville saw this in the America of his day: "The will of man is not shattered, but softened, bent, and guided. Men are seldom forced . . . to act, but they are constantly restrained from acting." As Ralph Barton Perry put it, "Whoever determines what alternatives shall be made known to man controls what that man shall choose *from*. He is deprived of freedom in proportion as he is denied access to *any* ideas, or is confined to any range of ideas short of the totality of relevant possibilities." For "deprived of freedom" read "controlled."

It is no doubt valuable to create an environment in which a person acquires effective behavior rapidly and continues to behave effectively. In constructing such an environment we may eliminate distractions and open opportunities, and these are key points in the metaphor of guidance or growth or development; but it is the contingencies we arrange, rather than the unfolding of some predetermined pattern, which are responsible for the changes observed.

BUILDING DEPENDENCE ON THINGS

Jean-Jacques Rousseau was alert to the dangers of social control, and he thought it might be possible to avoid them by making a person dependent not on people but on things. In *Emile* he showed how a child could learn about things from the things themselves rather than from books. The practices he described are still common, largely because of John Dewey's emphasis on real life in the classroom.

One of the advantages in being dependent on things rather than on other people is that the time and energy of other people are saved. The child who must be reminded that it is time to go to school is dependent upon his parents, but the child who has learned to respond to clocks and other temporal properties of the world around him (not to a "sense of time") is dependent upon things, and he makes fewer demands on his parents. In learning to drive a car a person remains dependent on an instructor as long as he must be told when to apply the brakes, when to signal a turn, when to change speeds, and so on; when his behavior comes under the control of the natural consequences of driving a car, he may dispense with the instructor. Among the "things" upon which a person should become dependent are other people when they are not acting specifically to change his behavior. The child who must be told what to say and how to behave with respect to other people is dependent upon those who tell him; the child who has learned how to get along with other people can dispense with advice.

Another important advantage of being dependent on things is that the contingencies which involve things are more precise and shape more useful behavior than contingencies arranged by other people. The temporal properties of the environment are more pervasive and more subtle than any series of reminders. A person whose behavior in driving a car is shaped by the response of the car behaves more skillfully than one who is following instructions. Those who get along well with people as the result of direct exposure to social contingencies are more skillful than those who have merely been told what to say and do.

These are important advantages, and a world in which all behavior is dependent on things is an attractive prospect. In such a world everyone would behave well with respect to his fellow men as he had learned to do when exposed to their approval and disapproval; he would work productively and carefully and exchange things with others because of their natural values; and he would learn things which naturally interest him and which are naturally useful. All this would be better than behaving well by obeying the law as enforced by police, working productively for the contrived reinforcers called money, and studying to get marks and grades.

But things do not easily take control. The procedures Rousseau described were not simple, and they do not often work. The complex contingencies involving things (including people who are behaving "unintentionally") can, unaided, have very little effect on an individual in his lifetime—a fact of great importance for reasons we shall note later. We must also remember that the control exercised by things may be destructive. The world of things can be tyrannical. Natural contingencies induce people to behave superstitiously, to risk greater and greater dangers, to work uselessly to exhaustion, and so on. Only the counter-control exerted by a social environment offers any protection against these consequences.

Dependence on things is not independence. The child who does not need to be told that it is time to go to school has come under the control of more subtle, and more useful, stimuli. The child who has learned what to say and how to behave in getting along with other people is under the control of social contingencies. People who get along together well under

the mild contingencies of approval and disapproval
are controlled as effectively as (and in many ways
more effectively than) the citizens of a police state.
Orthodoxy controls through the establishment of rules,
but the mystic is no freer because the contingencies
which have shaped his behavior are more personal
or idiosyncratic. Those who work productively because of the reinforcing value of what they produce
are under the sensitive and powerful control of the
products. Those who learn in the natural environment
are under a form of control as powerful as any control exerted by a teacher.

A person never becomes truly self-reliant. Even
though he deals effectively with things, he is necessarily dependent upon those who have taught him to
do so. They have selected the things he is dependent
upon and determined the kinds and degrees of dependencies. (They cannot, therefore, disclaim responsibility for the results.)

Changing Minds

It is a surprising fact that those who object most violently to the manipulation of behavior nevertheless
make the most vigorous efforts to manipulate minds.
Evidently freedom and dignity are threatened only
when behavior is changed by physically changing the
environment. There appears to be no threat when the
states of mind said to be responsible for behavior are
changed, presumably because autonomous man possesses miraculous powers which enable him to yield
or resist.

It is fortunate that those who object to the manipulation of behavior feel free to manipulate minds, since
otherwise they would have to remain silent. But no

one directly changes a mind. By manipulating environmental contingencies, one makes changes which are said to indicate a change of mind, but if there is any effect, it is on behavior. The control is inconspicuous and not very effective, and some control therefore seems to be retained by the person whose mind changes. A few characteristic ways of changing minds may be examined.

We sometimes induce a man to behave by prompting him (for example, when he is not able to solve a problem), or by suggesting a course of action (for example, when he is at a loss as to what to do). Prompts, hints, and suggestions are all stimuli, usually but not always verbal, and they have the important property of exerting only partial control. No one responds to a prompt, hint, or suggestion unless he already has some tendency to behave in a given way. When the contingencies which explain the prevailing tendency are not identified, some part of the behavior can be attributed to the mind. The inner control is particularly convincing when the external is not explicit, as when one tells an apparently irrelevant story which nevertheless serves as a prompt, hint, or suggestion. Setting an example exerts a similar kind of control, exploiting a general tendency to behave imitatively. Advertising testimonials "control the mind" in this way.

We also seem to be acting upon the mind when we *urge* a person to act or *persuade* him to act. Etymologically, to urge is to press or drive; it is to make an aversive situation more *urgent*. We urge a person to act as we might nudge him into acting. The stimuli are usually mild, but they are effective if they have been associated in the past with stronger aversive consequences. Thus, we urge on a dawdler by saying, "Look what time it is," and we succeed in inducing him to hurry if earlier delays have been punished. We urge a person not to spend money by pointing to his low bank balance, and we are effective if he has suffered when he has run out of money in the past. We *persuade* people, however, by pointing to stimuli associated with positive consequences. Etymologically, the word is related to sweeten. We persuade someone by making a situation more favorable for action, as by describing likely reinforcing consequences. Here again there is an apparent discrepancy between the strength of the stimuli we use and the magnitude of the effect. Urging and persuading are effective only if there is already some tendency to behave, and the behavior can be attributed to an inner man so long as that tendency is unexplained.

Beliefs, preferences, perceptions, needs, purposes, and opinions are other possessions of autonomous man which are said to change when we change minds. What is changed in each case is a probability of action. A person's belief that a floor will hold him as he walks across it depends upon his past experience. If he has walked across it without incident many times, he will do so again readily, and his behavior will not create any of the aversive stimuli felt as anxiety. He may report that he has "faith" in the solidity of the floor or "confidence" that it will hold him, but the kinds of things which are felt as faith or confidence are not states of mind; they are at best by-products of the behavior in its relation to antecedent events, and they do not explain why a person walks as he does.

We build "belief" when we increase the probability of action by reinforcing behavior. When we build a person's confidence that a floor will hold him by inducing him to walk on it, we might not be said to be changing a belief, but we do so in the traditional sense when we give him verbal assurances that the

Beyond Freedom and Dignity   89

floor is solid, demonstrate its solidity by walking on
it ourselves, or describe its structure or state. The only
difference is in the conspicuousness of the measures.
The change which occurs as a person "learns to trust
a floor" by walking on it is the characteristic effect
of reinforcement; the change which occurs when he
is told that the floor is solid, when he sees someone
else walking on it, or when he is "convinced" by assurances that the floor will hold him depends upon
past experiences which no longer make a conspicuous
contribution. For example, a person who walks on
surfaces which are likely to vary in their solidity (for
example, a frozen lake) quickly forms a discrimination
between surfaces on which others are walking and
surfaces on which no one is walking, or between surfaces called safe and surfaces called dangerous. He
learns to walk confidently on the first and cautiously
on the second. The sight of someone walking on a
surface or an assurance that it is safe converts it from
the second class into the first. The history during which
the discrimination was formed may be forgotten, and
the effect then seems to involve that inner event called
a change of mind.

Changes in preference, perceptions, needs, purposes, attitudes, opinions, and other attributes of mind
may be analyzed in the same way. We change the
way a person looks at something, as well as what he
sees when he looks, by changing the contingencies;
we do not change something called perception. We
change the relative strengths of responses by differential reinforcement of alternative courses of action;
we do not change something called a preference. We
change the probability of an act by changing a condition of deprivation or aversive stimulation; we do
not change a need. We reinforce behavior in particular
ways; we do not give a person a purpose or an inten-

tion. We change behavior toward something, not an attitude toward it. We sample and change verbal behavior, not opinions.

Another way to change a mind is to point to reasons why a person should behave in a given way, and the reasons are almost always consequences which are likely to be contingent on behavior. Let us say that a child is using a knife in a dangerous way. We may avoid trouble by making the environment safer—by taking the knife away or giving him a safer kind—but that will not prepare him for a world with unsafe knives. Left alone, he may learn to use the knife properly by cutting himself whenever he uses it improperly. We may help by substituting a less dangerous form of punishment—spanking him, for example, or perhaps merely shaming him when we find him using a knife in a dangerous way. We may tell him that some uses are bad and others good if "Bad!" and "Good!" have already been conditioned as positive and negative reinforcers. Suppose, however, that all these methods have unwanted by-products, such as a change in his relation to us, and that we therefore decide to appeal to "reason." (This is possible, of course, only if he has reached the "age of reason.") We explain the contingencies, demonstrating what happens when one uses a knife in one way and not another. We may show him how rules may be extracted from the contingencies ("You should never cut *toward yourself*"). As a result we may induce the child to use the knife properly and will be likely to say that we have imparted a knowledge of its proper use. But we have had to take advantage of a great deal of prior conditioning with respect to instructions, directions, and other verbal stimuli, which are easily overlooked, and their contribution may then be attributed to autonomous man. A still more complex form of argument has to do with deriving new reasons from old, the process of deduction which depends upon a much longer verbal history and is particularly likely to be called changing a mind.

Ways of changing behavior by changing minds are seldom condoned when they are clearly effective, even though it is still a mind which is apparently being changed. We do not condone the changing of minds when the contestants are unevenly matched; that is "undue influence." Nor do we condone changing minds surreptitiously. If a person cannot see what the would-be changer of minds is doing, he cannot escape or counterattack; he is being exposed to "propaganda." "Brainwashing" is proscribed by those who otherwise condone the changing of minds simply because the control is obvious. A common technique is to build up a strong aversive condition, such as hunger or lack of sleep and, by alleviating it, to reinforce any behavior which "shows a positive attitude" toward a political or religious system. A favorable "opinion" is built up simply by reinforcing favorable statements. The procedure may not be obvious to those upon whom it is used, but it is too obvious to others to be accepted as an allowable way of changing minds.

The illusion that freedom and dignity are respected when control seems incomplete arises in part from the probabilistic nature of operant behavior. Seldom does any environmental condition "elicit" behavior in the all-or-nothing fashion of a reflex; it simply makes a bit of behavior more likely to occur. A hint will not itself suffice to evoke a response, but it adds strength to a weak response which may then appear. The hint is conspicuous, but the other events responsible for the appearance of the response are not.

Like permissiveness, maieutics, guidance, and building a dependence on things, changing a mind is con-

doned by the defenders of freedom and dignity because it is an ineffective way of changing behavior,
and the changer of minds can therefore escape from
the charge that he is controlling people. He is also
exonerated when things go wrong. Autonomous man
survives to be credited with his achievements and
blamed for his mistakes.

The apparent freedom respected by weak measures
is merely inconspicuous control. When we seem to
turn control over to a person himself, we simply
shift from one mode of control to another. A news
weekly, discussing the legal control of abortion, contended that "the way to deal with the problem forth-
rightly is on terms that permit the individual, guided
by conscience and intelligence, to make a choice un-
hampered by archaic and hypocritical concepts and
statutes." What is recommended is not a shift from
legal control to "choice" but to the control previously
exerted by religious, ethical, governmental, and educational agencies. The individual is "permitted" to
decide the issue for himself simply in the sense that
he will act because of consequences to which legal
punishment is no longer to be added.

A permissive government is a government that leaves
control to other sources. If people behave well under
it, it is because they have been brought under effective
ethical control or the control of things, or have been
induced by educational and other agencies to behave
in loyal, patriotic, and law-abiding ways. Only when
other forms of control are available is that government
best which governs least. To the extent that government is defined by the power to punish, the literature
of freedom has been valuable in promoting a shift to
other measures, but in no other sense has it freed
people from governmental control.

A free economy does not mean the absence of economic control, because no economy is free as long as goods and money remain reinforcing. When we refuse to impose control over wages, prices, and the use of natural resources in order not to interfere with individual initiative, we leave the individual under the control of unplanned economic contingencies. Nor is any school "free." If the teacher does not teach, students will learn only if less explicit but still effective contingencies prevail. The nondirective psychotherapist may free his patient from certain harmful contingencies in his daily life, but the patient will "find his own solution" only if ethical, governmental, religious, educational, or other contingencies induce him to do so.

(The contact between therapist and patient is a sensitive subject. The therapist, no matter how "nondirective," sees his patient, talks with him, and listens to him. He is professionally concerned for his welfare, and if he is sympathetic, he *cares* for him. All this is reinforcing. It has been suggested, however, that the therapist can avoid changing his patient's behavior if he makes these reinforcers noncontingent—that is, if they are not permitted to follow any particular form of behavior. As one writer has put it, "The therapist responds as a congruent person, with sensitive empathy and unqualified caring that, in learning theory terms, rewards the client as much for one behavior as for any other." This is probably an impossible assignment and in any case would not have the effect claimed. Noncontingent reinforcers are not ineffective; a reinforcer always reinforces something. When a therapist shows that he cares, he reinforces any behavior the patient has just emitted. One reinforcement, accidental though it may be, strengthens behavior which is then more likely to occur and be reinforced again. The resulting "superstition" can be demonstrated in pigeons, and it is unlikely that men have become less sensitive to adventitious reinforcement. Being good to someone for no reason at all, treating him affectionately whether he is good or bad, does have Biblical support: grace must not be contingent upon works or it is no longer grace. But there are behavioral processes to be taken into account.)

The fundamental mistake made by all those who choose weak methods of control is to assume that the balance of control is left to the individual, when in fact it is left to other conditions. The other conditions are often hard to see, but to continue to neglect them and to attribute their effects to autonomous man is to court disaster. When practices are concealed or disguised, countercontrol is made difficult; it is not clear from whom one is to escape or whom one is to attack. The literatures of freedom and dignity were once brilliant exercises in countercontrol, but the measures they proposed are no longer appropriate to the task. On the contrary, they may have serious consequences, to which we must now turn.

* * *

The freedom and dignity of autonomous man seem to be preserved when only weak forms of nonaversive control are used. Those who use them seem to defend themselves against the charge that they are attempting to control behavior, and they are exonerated when things go wrong Permissiveness is the absence of control, and if it appears to lead to desirable results, it is only because of other contingencies. Maieutics, or the art of midwifery, seems to leave behavior to be credited to those who give birth to it, and the guidance of development to those who develop. Human intervention seems to be minimized when a person is made dependent upon things rather than upon other people. Various ways of changing behavior by changing minds are not only condoned but vigorously practiced by the defenders of freedom and dignity. There is a good deal to be said for minimizing current control by other people, but other measures still operate. A person who responds in acceptable ways to weak forms of control may have been changed by contingencies which are no longer operative. By refusing to recognize them the defenders of freedom and dignity encourage the misuse of controlling practices and block progress toward a more effective technology of behavior.

6
Values

IN WHAT WE MAY CALL the prescientific view (and the word is not necessarily pejorative) a person's behavior is at least to some extent his own achievement. He is free to deliberate, decide, and act, possibly in original ways, and he is to be given credit for his successes and blamed for his failures. In the scientific view (and the word is not necessarily honorific) a person's behavior is determined by a genetic endowment traceable to the evolutionary history of the species and by the environmental circumstances to which as an individual he has been exposed. Neither view can be proved, but it is in the nature of scientific inquiry that the evidence should shift in favor of the second. As we learn more about the effects of the environment, we have less reason to attribute any part of human behavior to an autonomous controlling agent. And the second view shows a marked advantage when we begin to do something about behavior. Autonomous man is not easily changed; in fact, to the extent that he is autonomous, he is by definition not changeable at all. But the environment can be changed, and we are learning how to change it. The measures we use are those of physical and biological technology, but we use them in special ways to affect behavior.

Something is missing in this shift from internal to external control. Internal control is presumably exerted not only by but for autonomous man. But for whom is a powerful technology of behavior to be used? Who is to use it? And to what end? We have been implying that the effects of one practice are better than those of another, but on what grounds? What is the good against which something else is called better? Can we define the good life? Or progress toward a good life? Indeed, what is progress? What, in a word, is the meaning of life, for the individual or the species?

Questions of this sort seem to point toward the future, to be concerned not with man's origins but with his destiny. They are said, of course, to involve "value judgments"—to raise questions not about facts but about how men feel about facts, not about what man *can* do but about what he *ought* to do. It is usually implied that the answers are out of reach of science. Physicists and biologists often agree, and with some justification, since their sciences do not, indeed, have the answers. Physics may tell us how to build a nuclear bomb but not whether it should be built. Biology may tell us how to control birth and postpone death but not whether we ought to do so. Decisions about the uses of science seem to demand a kind of wisdom which, for some curious reason, scientists are denied. If they are to make value judgments at all, it is only with the wisdom they share with people in general.

It would be a mistake for the behavioral scientist to agree. How people feel about facts, or what it means to feel anything, is a question for which a science of behavior should have an answer. A fact is no doubt different from what a person feels about it, but the latter is a fact also. What causes trouble, here as elsewhere, is the appeal to what people feel. A more useful form of the question is this: If a scientific analysis can tell us how to change behavior, can it tell us what changes to make? This is a question about the behavior of those who do in fact propose and make changes. People act to improve the world and to progress to-

ward a better way of life for good reasons, and among
the reasons are certain consequences of their behavior,
and among these consequences are the things people
value and call good.

We may begin with some simple examples. There are
things which almost everyone calls good. Some things
taste good, feel good, or look good. We say this as
readily as we say that they taste sweet, feel rough, or
look red. Is there then some physical property possessed by all good things? Almost certainly not. There
is not even any common property possessed by all
sweet, rough, or red things. A gray surface looks red
if we have been looking at a blue-green one; plain
paper feels smooth if we have been feeling sandpaper
or rough if we have been feeling plate glass; and tap
water tastes sweet if we have been eating artichokes.
Some part of what we call red or smooth or sweet must
therefore be in the eyes or fingertips or tongue of the
beholder, feeler, or taster. What we attribute to an
object when we call it red, rough, or sweet is in part a
condition of our own body, resulting (in these examples) from recent stimulation. Conditions of the body
are much more important, and for a different reason,
when we call something good.

Good things are positive reinforcers. The food that
tastes good reinforces us when we taste it. Things that
feel good reinforce us when we feel them. Things that
look good reinforce us when we look at them. When
we say colloquially that we "go for" such things, we
identify a kind of behavior which is frequently reinforced by them. (The things we call bad also have no
common property. They are all negative reinforcers,
and we are reinforced when we escape from or avoid
them.)

When we say that a value judgment is a matter not

of fact but of how someone feels about a fact, we are simply distinguishing between a thing and its reinforcing effect. Things themselves are studied by physics and biology, usually without reference to their value, but the reinforcing effects of things are the province of behavioral science, which, to the extent that it is concerned with operant reinforcement, is a science of values.

Things are good (positively reinforcing) or bad (negatively reinforcing) presumably because of the contingencies of survival under which the species evolved. There is obvious survival value in the fact that certain foods are reinforcing; it has meant that men have more quickly learned to find, grow, or catch them. A susceptibility to negative reinforcement is equally important; those who have been most highly reinforced when they have escaped from or avoided potentially dangerous conditions have enjoyed obvious advantages. As a result it is part of the genetic endowment called "human nature" to be reinforced in particular ways by particular things. (It is also part of that endowment that new stimuli become reinforcing through "respondent" conditioning—that the sight of fruit, for example, becomes reinforcing if, after looking at the fruit, we bite into it and find it good. The possibility of respondent conditioning does not change the fact that all reinforcers eventually derive their power from evolutionary selection.)

To make a value judgment by calling something good or bad is to classify it in terms of its reinforcing effects. The classification is important, as we shall see in a moment, when reinforcers begin to be used by other people (when, for example, the verbal responses "Good!" and "Bad!" begin to function as reinforcers), but things were reinforcing long before they were called good or bad—and they are still reinforcing to animals who do not call them good or bad and to babies and other people who are not able to do so. The reinforcing effect is the important thing, but is this what is meant by "the way men feel about things"? Are things not reinforcing *because* they feel good or bad?

Feelings are said to be part of the armamentarium of autonomous man, and some further comment is in order. A person feels things within his body as he feels things on its surface. He feels a lame muscle as he feels a slap on the face, he feels depressed as he feels a cold wind. Two important differences arise from the difference in location. In the first place, he can feel things outside his skin in an active sense; he can feel a surface by running his fingers over it to enrich the stimulation he receives from it, but even though there are ways in which he can "heighten his awareness" of the things inside his body, he does not actively feel them in the same way.

A more important difference is in the way a person learns to feel things. A child learns to distinguish among different colors, tones, odors, tastes, temperatures, and so on only when they enter into contingencies of reinforcement. If red candies have a reinforcing flavor and green candies do not, the child takes and eats red candies. Some important contingencies are verbal. Parents teach a child to name colors by reinforcing correct responses. If the child says "Blue" and the object before him is blue, the parent says "Good!" or "Right!" If the object is red, the parent says "Wrong!" This is not possible when the child is learning to respond to things inside his body. A person who is teaching a child to distinguish among his feelings is a little like a color-blind person teaching a child to name colors. The teacher cannot be sure of the presence or absence of the condition which determines whether a response is to be reinforced or not.

In general the verbal community cannot arrange the subtle contingencies necessary to teach fine distinctions among stimuli which are inaccessible to it. It must rely on visible evidence of the presence or absence of a private condition. A parent may teach a child to say "I am hungry" not because he feels what the child is feeling, but because he sees him eating ravenously or behaving in some other way related to deprivation of, or reinforcement with, food. The evidence may be good, and the child may learn to "describe his feelings" with some accuracy, but this is by no means always the case, because many feelings have inconspicuous behavioral manifestations. As a result the language of emotion is not precise. We tend to describe our emotions with terms which have been learned in connection with other kinds of things; almost all the words we use were originally metaphors.

We may teach a child to call things good by reinforcing him according to how they taste, look, or feel *to us*, but not everyone finds the same things good, and we can be wrong. The only other available evidence is from the child's behavior. If we give a child a new food and he begins to eat it actively, the first taste has obviously been reinforcing, and we then tell him that the food is good and agree with him when he calls it good. But the child has other information. He feels other effects, and later he will call other things good if they have the same effects, even though active eating is not among them.

There is no important causal connection between the reinforcing effect of a stimulus and the feelings to which it gives rise. We might be tempted to say, following William James' reinterpretation of emotion, that a stimulus is not reinforcing because it feels good

but feels good because it is reinforcing. But the "because's" are again misleading. Stimuli are reinforcing
and produce conditions which are felt as good for a
single reason, to be found in an evolutionary history.

Even as a clue, the important thing is not the feeling
but the thing felt. It is the glass that feels smooth, not
a "feeling of smoothness." It is the reinforcer that feels
good, not the good feeling. Men have generalized the
feelings of good things and called them pleasure and
the feelings of bad things and called them pain, but
we do not give a man pleasure or pain, we give him
things he feels as pleasant or painful. Men do not work
to maximize pleasure and minimize pain, as the hedo-
nists have insisted; they work to produce pleasant
things and to avoid painful things. Epicurus was not
quite right: pleasure is not the ultimate good, pain the
ultimate evil; the only good things are positive reinforcers, and the only bad things are negative reinforcers. What is maximized or minimized, or what is ulti-
mately good or bad, are things, not feelings, and men
work to achieve them or to avoid them not because of
the way they feel but because they are positive or negative reinforcers. (When we call something *pleasing*, we
may be reporting a feeling, but the feeling is a by-
product of the fact that a pleasing thing is quite literally a reinforcing thing. We speak of sensory *gratification* as if it were a matter of feelings, but to gratify is
to reinforce, and gratitude refers to reciprocal reinforcement. We call a reinforcer *satisfying*, as if we
were reporting a feeling; but the word literally refers
to a change in the state of deprivation which makes an
object reinforcing. To be satisfied is to be sated.)

Some of the simple goods which function as reinforcers
come from other people. People keep warm or safe by
keeping close together, they reinforce each other sexu-

ally, and they share, borrow, or steal each other's possessions. Reinforcement by another person need not be intentional. One person learns to clap his hands to attract the attention of another, but the other does not turn in order to induce him to clap again. A mother learns to calm a disturbed child by caressing him, but the child does not become silent to induce her to caress him again. A man learns to drive away an enemy by striking him, but the enemy does not depart to induce him to strike on another occasion. In each case we call the reinforcing action unintentional. It becomes intentional if the effect is reinforcing. A person acts intentionally, as we have seen, not in the sense that he possesses an intention which he then carries out, but in the sense that his behavior has been strengthened by consequences. A child who cries until caressed begins to cry intentionally. A boxing instructor may teach his pupil to strike him in a given way by acting as if hurt. One person is not likely to attend to another in order to induce him to clap his hands, but he may do so intentionally if that way of having one's attention called is less aversive than another.

When other people intentionally arrange and maintain contingencies of reinforcement, the person affected by the contingencies may be said to be behaving "for the good of others." Probably the first, and still the commonest, contingencies generating such behavior are aversive. Anyone who has the necessary power can treat others aversively until they respond in ways that reinforce him. Methods using positive reinforcement are harder to learn and less likely to be used because the results are usually deferred, but they have the advantage of avoiding counterattack. Which method is used often depends upon the available power: the strong threaten physical harm, the ugly frighten, the physically attractive reinforce sexually, and the wealthy pay. Verbal reinforcers derive their power from the specific reinforcers with which they are used, and since they are used with different reinforcers from time to time, the effect may be generalized. We reinforce a person positively by saying "Good!" or "Right!" and negatively by saying "Bad!" or "Wrong!" and these verbal stimuli are effective because they have been accompanied by other reinforcers.

(A distinction may be made between the two pairs of words. Behavior is called good or bad—and the ethical overtones are not accidents—according to the way in which it is usually reinforced by others. Behavior is usually called right or wrong with respect to other contingencies. There is a right and a wrong way to do something; a given move in driving a car is right rather than merely good and another move wrong rather than merely bad. A similar distinction may be made between praise and reproof on the one hand and credit and blame on the other. We praise and reprove people in general when their behavior is positively or negatively reinforcing to us, with no reference to the products of their behavior, but when we give a man credit *for* an achievement or blame him *for* trouble, we point to the achievement or the trouble and emphasize that they are indeed the consequences of his behavior. We use "Right!" and "Good!" almost interchangeably, however, and the distinction between praising and giving credit is perhaps not always worth making.)

The effect of a reinforcer which cannot be attributed to its survival value in the course of evolution (the effect of heroin, for example) is presumably anomalous. Conditioned reinforcers may seem to suggest other kinds of susceptibilities, but they are effective because of circumstances in a person's earlier history. According to Dodds, the Homeric Greek fought with inspired zeal to achieve not happiness but the esteem of his fellow men. Happiness may be taken to represent the personal reinforcers which can be attributed to survival value and esteem some of the conditioned reinforcers used to induce a person to behave for the good of others, but all conditioned reinforcers derive their power from personal reinforcers (in traditional terms, public interest is always based on private interest) and hence from the evolutionary history of the species.

How one feels about behaving for the good of others depends upon the reinforcers used. Feelings are by-products of the contingencies and throw no further light on the distinction between public and private. We do not say that simple biological reinforcers are effective because of self-love, and we should not attribute behaving for the good of others to a love of others. In working for the good of others a person may feel love or fear, loyalty or obligation, or any other condition arising from the contingencies responsible for the behavior. A person does not act for the good of others because of a feeling of belongingness or refuse to act because of feelings of alienation. His behavior depends upon the control exerted by the social environment.

When one person is induced to act for the good of another, we may ask whether the result is fair or just. Are the goods received by the two parties commensurate? When one person controls another aversively, there is no commensurate good, and positive reinforcers may also be used in such a way that the gains are far from equal. Nothing in the behavioral processes guarantees fair treatment, since the amount of behavior generated by a reinforcer depends upon the contingencies in which it appears. In an extreme case a person may be reinforced by others on a schedule which

costs him his life. Suppose, for example, that a group
is threatened by a predator (the "monster" of mythol-
ogy). Someone possessing special strength or skill attacks and kills the monster or drives him away. The
group, released from threat, reinforces the hero with
approval, praise, honor, affection, celebrations, statues,
arches of triumph, and the hand of the princess. Some
of this may be unintentional, but it is nevertheless
reinforcing to the hero. Some may be intentional—that
is, the hero is reinforced precisely to induce him to
take on other monsters. The important fact about such
contingencies is that the greater the threat, the greater
the esteem accorded the hero who alleviates it. The
hero therefore takes on more and more dangerous as-
signments until he is killed. The contingencies are not
necessarily social; they are found in other dangerous
activities such as mountain climbing, where the release
from threat becomes more reinforcing the greater the
threat. (That a behavioral process should thus go
wrong and lead to death is no more a violation of the
principle of natural selection than the phototropic behavior of the moth, which has survival value when it
leads the moth into sunlight but proves lethal when
it leads into flame.)

As we have seen, the issue of fairness or justice is
often simply a matter of good husbandry. The question
is whether reinforcers are being used wisely. Two other
words long associated with value judgments but not
so clearly a matter of husbandry are "should" and
"ought." We use them to clarify nonsocial contingencies. "To get to Boston you should (you ought to)
follow Route 1" is simply a way of saying "If you will
be reinforced by reaching Boston, you will be reinforced if you follow Route 1." To say that following
Route 1 is the "right" way to get to Boston is not an
ethical or moral judgment but a statement about a

highway system. Something closer to a value judgment may seem to be present in such an expression as "You should (you ought to) read *David Copperfield*," which may be translated, "You will be reinforced if you read *David Copperfield*." It is a value judgment to the extent that it implies that the book will be reinforcing. We can bring the implication into the open by mentioning some of our evidence: "If you enjoyed *Great Expectations*, you should (you ought to) read *David Copperfield*." This value judgment is correct if it is generally true that those who are reinforced by *Great Expectations* are also reinforced by *David Copperfield*.

"Should" and "ought" begin to raise more difficult questions when we turn to the contingencies under which a person is induced to behave for the good of others. "You should (you ought to) tell the truth" is a value judgment to the extent that it refers to reinforcing contingencies. We might translate it as follows: "If you are reinforced by the approval of your fellow men, you will be reinforced when you tell the truth." The value is to be found in the social contingencies maintained for purposes of control. It is an ethical or moral judgment in the sense that ethos and mores refer to the customary practices of a group.

This is an area in which it is easy to lose sight of the contingencies. A person drives a car well because of the contingencies of reinforcement which have shaped and which maintain his behavior. The behavior is traditionally explained by saying that he possesses the knowledge or skill needed to drive a car, but the knowledge and skill must then be traced to contingencies that might have been used to explain the behavior in the first place. We do not say that a person does what he "ought to do" in driving a car because of any inner sense of what is right. We are likely to appeal to some such inner virtue, however, to explain why a person behaves well with respect to his fellow men, but he does so not because his fellow men have endowed him with a sense of responsibility or obligation or with loyalty or respect for others but because they have arranged effective social contingencies. The behaviors classified as good or bad and right or wrong are not due to goodness or badness, or a good or bad character, or a knowledge of right and wrong; they are due to contingencies involving a great variety of reinforcers, including the generalized verbal reinforcers of "Good!" "Bad!" "Right!" and "Wrong!"

Once we have identified the contingencies that control the behavior called good or bad and right or wrong, the distinction between facts and how people feel about facts is clear. How people feel about facts is a by-product. The important thing is what they do about them, and what they do is a fact that is to be understood by examining relevant contingencies. Karl Popper has stated a contrary traditional position as follows:

In face of the sociological fact that most people adopt the norm "Thou shalt not steal," it is still possible to decide to adopt either this norm, or its opposite; and it is possible to encourage those who have adopted the norm to hold fast to it, or to discourage them, and to persuade them to adopt another norm. *It is impossible to derive a sentence stating a norm or a decision from a sentence stating a fact;* this is only another way of saying that it is impossible to derive norms or decisions from facts.

The conclusion is valid only if indeed it is "possible to adopt a norm or its opposite." Here is autonomous man playing his most awe-inspiring role, but whether or not a person obeys the norm "Thou shalt not steal" depends upon supporting contingencies, which must not be overlooked.

Some relevant facts may be cited. Long before anyone formulated the "norm," people attacked those who
stole from them. At some point stealing came to be
called wrong and as such was punished even by those
who had not been robbed. Someone familiar with these
contingencies, possibly from having been exposed to
them, could then advise another person: "Don't steal."
If he had sufficient prestige or authority, he would not
need to describe the contingencies further. The stronger
form, "Thou shalt not steal," as one of the Ten Commandments, suggests supernatural sanctions. Relevant
social contingencies are implied by "You ought not to
steal," which could be translated, "If you tend to avoid
punishment, avoid stealing," or "Stealing is wrong, and
wrong behavior is punished." Such a statement is no
more normative than "If coffee keeps you awake when
you want to go to sleep, don't drink it."

A rule or law includes a statement of prevailing contingencies, natural or social. One may follow a rule or
obey a law simply because of the contingencies to
which the rule or law refers, but those who formulate
rules and laws usually supply additional contingencies.
A construction worker follows a rule by wearing a hard
hat. The natural contingencies, which involve protection from falling objects, are not very effective, and the
rule must therefore be enforced: those who do not
wear hard hats will be discharged. There is no *natural*
connection between wearing a hard hat and keeping
a job; the contingency is maintained to support the
natural but less effective contingencies involving protection from falling objects. A parallel argument could
be made for any rule involving social contingencies.
In the long run people behave more effectively if they
have been told the truth, but the gains are too remote
to affect the truthteller, and additional contingencies
are needed to maintain the behavior. Telling the truth

is therefore called good. It is the right thing to do, and
telling lies is bad and wrong. The "norm" is simply a
statement of the contingencies.

Intentional control "for the good of others" becomes
more powerful when it is exercised by religious, governmental, economic, and educational organizations. A
group maintains some kind of order by punishing its
members when they misbehave, but when this function
is taken over by a government, punishment is assigned
to specialists, to whom more powerful forms such as
fines, imprisonment, or death are available. "Good"
and "bad" become "legal" and "illegal," and the contingencies are codified in laws specifying behavior and
contingent punishments. Laws are useful to those who
must obey them because they specify the behavior
to be avoided, and they are useful to those who enforce
them because they specify the behavior to be punished.
The group is replaced by a much more sharply defined
agency—a state or nation—whose authority or power to
punish may be signalized with ceremonies, flags, music,
and stories about prestigious law-abiding citizens and
notorious lawbreakers.

A religious agency is a special form of government
under which "good" and "bad" become "pious" and
"sinful." Contingencies involving positive and negative
reinforcement, often of the most extreme sort, are codified—for example, as commandments—and maintained
by specialists, usually with the support of ceremonies,
rituals, and stories. Similarly, where the members of
an unorganized group exchange goods and services
under informal contingencies, an economic institution
or agency clarifies special roles—such as those of employer, worker, buyer, and seller—and constructs special types of reinforcers, such as money and credit
Contingencies are described in agreements, contracts,

and so on. Similarly, the members of an informal group learn from each other with or without intentional instruction, but organized education employs specialists called teachers, who operate in special places called schools, by arranging contingencies involving special reinforcers such as grades and diplomas. "Good" and "bad" become "right" and "wrong," and the behavior to be learned may be codified in syllabuses and tests.

As organized agencies induce people to behave "for the good of others" more effectively, they change what is felt. A person does not support his government because he is loyal but because the government has arranged special contingencies. We call him loyal and teach him to call himself loyal and to report any special conditions he may feel as "loyalty." A person does not support a religion because he is devout; he supports it because of the contingencies arranged by the religious agency. We call him devout and teach him to call himself devout and report what he feels as "devotion." Conflicts among feelings, as in the classical literary themes of love versus duty or patriotism versus faith, are really conflicts between contingencies of reinforcement.

As the contingencies which induce a man to behave "for the good of others" become more powerful, they overshadow contingencies involving personal reinforcers. They may then be challenged. Challenge is, of course, a metaphor which suggests a match or battle, and what people actually do in response to excessive or conflicting control can be more explicitly described. We saw the pattern in the struggle for freedom in Chapter 2. A person may defect from a government, turning to the informal control of a smaller group or to a Thoreauvian solitude. He may become an apostate from orthodox religion, turning to the ethical practices of an informal group or the seclusion of a hermitage. He may escape from organized economic control, turning to an informal exchange of goods and services or a solitary subsistence. He may abandon the organized knowledge of scholars and scientists, in favor of personal experience (turning from *Wissen* to *Verstehen*). Another possibility is to weaken or destroy those who impose the control, possibly by setting up a competing system.

These moves are often accompanied by verbal behavior which supports nonverbal action and induces others to participate. The value or validity of the reinforcers used by other people and by organized agencies may be questioned: "Why should I seek the admiration or avoid the censure of my fellow men?" "What can my government—or any government—really do to me?" "Can a church actually determine whether I am to be eternally damned or blessed?" "What is so wonderful about money—do I need all the things it buys?" "Why should I study the things set forth in a college catalogue?" In short, "Why should I behave 'for the good of others'?"

When the control exercised by others is thus evaded or destroyed, only the personal reinforcers are left. The individual turns to immediate gratification, possibly through sex or drugs. If he does not need to do much to find food, shelter, and safety, little behavior will be generated. His condition is then described by saying that he is suffering from a lack of values. As Maslow pointed out, valuelessness is "variously described as anomie, amorality, anhedonia, rootlessness, emptiness, hopelessness, the lack of something to believe in and be devoted to." These terms all seem to refer to feelings or states of mind, but what are missing are effective reinforcers. Anomie and amorality refer to a lack of the contrived reinforcers which induce people to observe rules. Anhedonia, rootlessness, emptiness, and hopelessness point to the absence of reinforcers of all kinds. The "something to believe in and be devoted to" is to be found among the contrived contingencies which induce people to behave "for the good of others."

The distinction between feelings and contingencies is particularly important when practical action must be taken. If the individual is indeed suffering from some internal state called valuelessness, then we can solve the problem only by altering that state—for example, by "reactivating moral power," "animating moral force," or "strengthening moral fiber or spiritual commitment." What must be changed are the contingencies, whether we regard them as responsible for the defective behavior or for the feelings said to explain the behavior.

A common proposal is to strengthen the original controls, eliminating conflicts, using stronger reinforcers, and sharpening the contingencies. If people do not work, it is not because they are lazy or shiftless but because they are not paid enough or because either welfare or affluence has made economic reinforcers less effective. The good things in life have only to be made properly contingent on productive labor. If citizens are not law-abiding, it is not because they are scofflaws or criminals but because law enforcement has grown lax; the problem can be solved by refusing to suspend or abridge sentences, by increasing the police force, and by passing stronger laws. If students do not study, it is not because they are not interested but because standards have been lowered or because the subjects taught are no longer relevant to a satisfactory life. Students will actively seek an education if the prestige accorded knowledge and skills is restored. (An incidental result will be that people will then *feel* industrious, law-abiding, and interested in getting an education.)

Such proposals to strengthen old modes of control are correctly called reactionary. The strategy may be successful, but it will not correct the trouble. Organized control "for the good of others" will continue to compete with personal reinforcers, and different kinds of organized control with each other. The balance of goods received by controller and controllee will remain unfair or unjust. If the problem is simply to correct the balance, any move which makes control more effective is in the wrong direction, but any move toward complete individualism or complete freedom from control is in the wrong direction too.

The first step in solving the problem is to identify all the goods received by the individual when he is controlled for the good of others. Other people exert control by manipulating the personal reinforcers to which the human organism is susceptible, together with conditioned reinforcers, such as praise or blame, derived from them. But there are other consequences which are easily overlooked because they do not occur immediately. We have already discussed the problem of making deferred aversive consequences effective. A similar problem arises when the deferred consequences are positively reinforcing. It is important enough to justify further comment.

The process of operant conditioning presumably evolved when those organisms which were more sensitively affected by the consequences of their behavior were better able to adjust to the environment and survive. Only fairly immediate consequences could be effective. One reason for this has to do with "final causes." Behavior cannot really be affected by anything which follows it, but if a "consequence" is immediate, it may overlap the behavior. A second reason has to do with the functional relation between behavior and its

consequences. The contingencies of survival could not
generate a process of conditioning which took into
account *how* behavior produced its consequences. The
only useful relation was temporal: a process could
evolve in which a reinforcer strengthened any behavior
it followed. But the process was important only if it
strengthened behavior which actually produced results.
Hence, the importance of the fact that any change that
follows closely upon a response is most likely to have
been produced by it. A third reason, related to the second but of a more practical nature, is that the reinforcing effect of any deferred consequence can be
usurped, so to speak, by intervening behavior, which
is reinforced even though it has had no part in the
production of the reinforcing event.

* * *

The process of operant conditioning is committed to
immediate effects, but remote consequences may be
important, and the individual gains if he can be brought
under their control. The gap can be bridged with a
series of "conditioned reinforcers," of which we have
already considered an example. A person who has frequently *escaped* from rain by moving under shelter
eventually *avoids* rain by moving before rain falls.
Stimuli which frequently precede rain become negative
reinforcers (we call them the sign or threat of rain).
They are more aversive when a person is not under
shelter, and by moving under shelter he *escapes* from
them and *avoids* getting wet. The effective consequence
is not that he does not get wet when rain eventually
falls but that a conditioned aversive stimulus is immediately reduced.

The mediation of a remote consequence is more easily
examined when the reinforcers are positive. Take, for
example, a bit of "paleobehavior" called banking a fire.

The practice of raking ashes over hot coals at night so that a live coal may be found in the morning to start another fire must have been very important when it was not easy to start a fire in any other way. How could it have been learned? (It is, of course, no explanation to say that someone "got the idea" of banking a fire, since we should have to pursue a similar line to explain the idea.) The live coal found in the morning could scarcely reinforce the behavior of raking ashes the night before, but the temporal gap could be bridged by a series of conditioned reinforcers. It is easy to learn to start a new fire from an old one which is not yet quite out, and if a fire has seemed to be out for some time, it should be easy to learn to dig into the ashes to find an ember. A deep pile of ashes would then become a conditioned reinforcer—the occasion upon which one may dig and find an ember. Raking ashes into a pile would then be automatically reinforced. The time span could at first have been very short—a fire was raked into a condition in which it was found shortly afterward—but as banking became a practice, the temporal aspects of the contingencies could have changed.

Like all accounts of the origins of paleobehavior, this is highly speculative, but it may serve to make a point. The contingencies under which people learned to bank fires must have been extremely rare. We must appeal for plausibility to the fact that there were hundreds of thousands of years during which they might have occurred. But once the behavior of banking a fire, or any part of it, had been acquired by one person, others could acquire it much more easily, and there was no further need for accidental contingencies.

One advantage in being a social animal is that one need not discover practices for oneself. The parent teaches his child, as the craftsman teaches his apprentice, because he gains a useful helper, but in the process the child and the apprentice acquire useful behavior which they would very probably not have acquired under nonsocial contingencies. Probably no one plants in the spring simply because he then harvests in the fall. Planting would not be adaptive or "reasonable" if there were no connection with a harvest, but one plants in the spring because of more immediate contingencies, most of them arranged by the social environment. The harvest has at best the effect of maintaining a series of conditioned reinforcers.

An important repertoire, necessarily acquired from others, is verbal. Verbal behavior presumably arose under contingencies involving practical social interactions, but the individual who becomes both a speaker and a listener is in possession of a repertoire of extraordinary scope and power, which he may use by himself. Parts of that repertoire are concerned with self-knowledge and self-control which, as we shall see in Chapter 9, are social products even though they are usually misrepresented as intensely individual and private things.

Still another advantage is that the individual is, after all, one of the "others" who exert control and who do so for their own benefit. Organized agencies are often justified by pointing to certain general values. The individual under a government enjoys a certain measure of *order* and *security*. An economic system justifies itself by pointing to the *wealth* it produces, and an educational establishment to *skills* and *knowledge*.

Without a social environment, a person remains essentially feral, like those children said to have been raised by wolves or to have been able to fend for themselves from an early age in a beneficent climate. A man who has been alone since birth will have no verbal behavior, will not be aware of himself as a person, will possess no techniques of self-management, and with respect to the world around him will have only those meager skills which can be acquired in one short lifetime from nonsocial contingencies. In Dante's hell, he will suffer the special tortures of those who "lived without blame and without praise," like the "angels who were . . . for themselves." To be for oneself is to be almost nothing.

The great individualists so often cited to show the value of personal freedom have owed their successes to earlier social environments. The involuntary individualism of a Robinson Crusoe and the voluntary individualism of a Henry David Thoreau show obvious debts to society. If Crusoe had reached the island as a baby, and if Thoreau had grown up unattended on the shores of Walden Pond, their stories would have been different. We must all begin as babies, and no degree of self-determination, self-sufficiency, or self-reliance will make us individuals in any sense beyond that of single members of the human species. Rousseau's great principle—that "nature has made man happy and good, but that society depraves him and makes him miserable" —was wrong, and it is ironic that in complaining that his book *Émile* was so little understood, Rousseau describes it as a "treatise on man's original goodness intended to show how vice and error, foreign to his nature, introduce themselves from without and insensibly change him," because the book is actually one of the great practical treatises on how human behavior can be changed.

Even those who stand out as revolutionaries are almost wholly the conventional products of the systems they overthrow. They speak the language, use the logic and science, observe many of the ethical and legal principles, and employ the practical skills and knowledge which society has given them. A small part of their behavior may be exceptional, possibly dramatically so, and we shall have to look for exceptional reasons in their idiosyncratic histories. (To attribute their original contributions to their miracle-working character as autonomous men is, of course, no explanation at all.)

These, then, are some of the gains to be credited to the control exerted by others in addition to the goods used in that control. The remoter gains are relevant to any evaluation of the justice or fairness of the exchange between the individual and his social environment. No reasonable balance can be achieved as long as the remoter gains are neglected by a thoroughgoing individualism or libertarianism, or as long as the balance is thrown as violently in the other direction by an exploitative system. Presumably, there is an optimal state of equilibrium in which everyone is maximally reinforced. But to say this is to introduce another kind of value. Why should anyone be concerned with justice or fairness, even if these can be reduced to good husbandry in the use of reinforcers? The questions with which we began obviously cannot be answered simply by pointing to what is personally good or what is good for others. There is another kind of value to which we must now turn.

*   *   *

The struggle for freedom and dignity has been formulated as a defense of autonomous man rather than as a revision of the contingencies of reinforcement under which people live. A technology of behavior is available which would more successfully reduce the aversive consequences of behavior, proximate or deferred, and maximize the achievements of which the human organism is capable, but the defenders of freedom oppose its use. The opposition may raise certain questions concerning "values." Who is to decide what is

good for man? How will a more effective technology
be used? By whom and to what end? These are really
questions about reinforcers. Some things have become
"good" during the evolutionary history of the species,
and they may be used to induce people to behave for
"the good of others." When used to excess, they may be
challenged, and the individual may turn to things good
only to him. The challenge may be answered by in-
tensifying the contingencies which generate behavior
for the good of others or by pointing to previously
neglected individual gains, such as those conceptual-
ized as security, order, health, wealth, or wisdom. Possibly indirectly, other people bring the individual under
the control of some remote consequences of his behavior, and the good of others then redounds to the
good of the individual. Another kind of good which
makes for human progress remains to be analyzed.

7
The Evolution of
a Culture

A CHILD IS BORN a member of the human species, with a genetic endowment showing many idiosyncratic features, and he begins at once to acquire a repertoire of behavior under the contingencies of reinforcement to which he is exposed as an individual. Most of these contingencies are arranged by other people. They are, in fact, what is called a culture, although the term is usually defined in other ways. Two eminent anthropologists have said, for example, that "the essential core of culture consists of traditional (i.e., historically derived and selected) ideas and especially their attached values." But those who observe cultures do not see ideas or values. They see how people live, how they raise their children, how they gather or cultivate food, what kinds of dwellings they live in, what they wear, what games they play, how they treat each other, how they govern themselves, and so on. These are the customs, the customary *behaviors*, of a people. To explain them we must turn to the contingencies which generate them.

Some contengencies are part of the physical environment, but they usually work in combination with social contingencies, and the latter are naturally emphasized by those who study cultures. The social contingencies, or the behaviors they generate, are the "ideas" of a culture; the reinforcers that appear in the contingencies are its "values."

A person is not only exposed to the contingencies that constitute a culture, he helps to maintain them, and to the extent that the contingencies induce him to do so the culture is self-perpetuating. The effective reinforcers are a matter of observation and cannot be disputed. What a given group of people calls good is a fact: it is what members of the group find reinforcing as the result of their genetic endowment and the natural and social contingencies to which they have been exposed. Each culture has its own set of goods, and what is good in one culture may not be good in another. To recognize this is to take the position of "cultural relativism." What is good for the Trobriand Islander is good for the Trobriand Islander, and that is that. Anthropologists have often emphasized relativism as a tolerant alternative to missionary zeal in converting all cultures to a single set of ethical, governmental, religious, or economic values.

A given set of values may explain why a culture functions, possibly without much change for a long time; but no culture is in permanent equilibrium. Contingencies necessarily change. The physical environment changes, as people move about, as the climate changes, as natural resources are consumed or diverted to other uses or made unusable, and so on. Social contingencies also change as the size of a group or its contact with other groups changes, or as controlling agencies grow more or less powerful or compete among themselves, or as the control exerted leads to countercontrol in the form of escape or revolt. The contingencies characteristic of a culture may not be adequately transmitted, so that the tendency to be reinforced by a given set of values is not maintained. The margin of safety in dealing with emergencies may then be narrowed or broadened. In short, the culture may grow stronger or weaker, and we may foresee that it will survive or perish. The survival of a culture then emerges as a new value to be taken into account in addition to personal and social goods.

The fact that a culture may survive or perish suggests a kind of evolution, and a parallel with the evolution of species has, of course, often been pointed out. It needs to be stated carefully. A culture corresponds to a species. We describe it by listing many of its practices, as we describe a species by listing many of its anatomical features. Two or more cultures may share a practice, as two or more species may share an anatomical feature. The practices of a culture, like the characteristics of a species, are carried by its members, who transmit them to other members. In general, the greater the number of individuals who carry a species or a culture, the greater its chance of survival.

A culture, like a species, is selected by its adaptation to an environment: to the extent that it helps its members to get what they need and avoid what is dangerous, it helps them to survive and transmit the culture. The two kinds of evolution are closely interwoven. The same people transmit both a culture and a genetic endowment—though in very different ways and for different parts of their lives. The capacity to undergo the changes in behavior which make a culture possible was acquired in the evolution of the species, and, reciprocally, the culture determines many of the biological characteristics transmitted. Many current cultures, for example, enable individuals to survive and breed who would otherwise fail to do so. Not every practice in a culture, or every trait in a species, is adaptive, since nonadaptive practices and traits may be carried by adaptive ones, and cultures and species which are poorly adaptive may survive for a long time.

New practices correspond to genetic mutations. A new practice may weaken a culture—for example, by leading to an unnecessary consumption of resources or by impairing the health of its members—or strengthen it—for example, by helping its members make a more effective use of resources or improve their health. Just as a mutation, a change in the structure of a gene, is unrelated to the contingencies of selection which affect the resulting trait, so the origin of a practice need not be related to its survival value. The food allergy of a strong leader may give rise to a dietary law, a sexual idiosyncrasy to a marriage practice, the character of a terrain to a military strategy—and the practices may be valuable to the culture for quite unrelated reasons. Many cultural practices have, of course, been traced to accidents. Early Rome, situated on a fertile plain and raided by tribes from the natural fortresses of the surrounding hills, developed laws concerning property which outlasted the original problem. The Egyptians, reconstructing boundaries after the annual flooding of the Nile, developed trigonometry, which proved valuable for many other reasons.

The parallel between biological and cultural evolution breaks down at the point of transmission. There is nothing like the chromosome-gene mechanism in the transmission of a cultural practice. Cultural evolution is Lamarckian in the sense that acquired practices are transmitted. To use a well-worn example, the giraffe does not stretch its neck to reach food which is otherwise out of reach and then pass on a longer neck to its offspring; instead, those giraffes in whom mutation has produced longer necks are more likely to reach available food and transmit the mutation. But a culture which develops a practice permitting it to use otherwise inaccessible sources of food can transmit that practice not only to new members but to contemporaries or to surviving members of an earlier generation. More important, a practice can be transmitted through "diffusion" to other cultures—as if antelopes, observing the usefulness of the long neck in giraffes, were to grow longer necks. Species are isolated from each other by the nontransmissibility of genetic traits, but there is no comparable isolation of cultures. A culture is a set of practices, but it is not a set which cannot be mixed with other sets.

We tend to associate a culture with a group of people. People are easier to see than their behavior, and behavior is easier to see than the contingencies which generate it. (Also easy to see, and hence often invoked in defining a culture, are the language spoken and the things the culture uses, such as tools, weapons, clothing, and art forms.) Only to the extent that we identify a culture with the people who practice it can we speak of a "member of a culture," since one cannot be a member of a set of contingencies of reinforcement or of a set of artifacts (or, for that matter, of "a set of ideas and their associated values").

Several kinds of isolation may produce a well-defined culture by limiting the transmissibility of practices. Geographical isolation is suggested when we speak of a "Samoan" culture, and racial characteristics which may interfere with the exchange of practices by a "Polynesian" culture. A dominant controlling agency or system may hold a set of practices together. A democratic culture, for example, is a social environment marked by certain governmental practices, supported by compatible ethical, religious, economic, and educational practices. A Christian, Moslem, or Buddhist culture suggests a dominant religious control, and a capitalist or socialist culture a dominant set of economic practices, each possibly associated with compatible practices of other kinds. A culture defined by a government, a religion, or an economic system does not require geographical or racial isolation.

Although the parallel between biological and cultural evolution falters at the point of transmissibility, the notion of cultural evolution remains useful. New practices arise, and they tend to be transmitted if they contribute to the survival of those who practice them. We can in fact trace the evolution of a culture more clearly than the evolution of a species, since the essential conditions are observed rather than inferred and can often be directly manipulated. Nevertheless, as we have seen, the role of the environment has only begun to be understood, and the social environment which is a culture is often hard to identify. It is constantly changing, it lacks substance, and it is easily confused with the people who maintain the environment and are affected by it.

Since a culture tends to be identified with the people who practice it, the principle of evolution has been used to justify competition between cultures in the so-called "doctrine of Social Darwinism." Wars between governments, religions, economic systems, races, and classes have been defended on the grounds that the survival of the fittest is a law of nature—and a nature "red in tooth and claw." If man has emerged as a master species, why should we not look forward to a master subspecies or race? If culture has evolved in a similar process, why not a master culture? It is true that people do kill each other, and often because of practices which seem to define cultures. One government or form of government competes with another, and the principal means are indicated by their military budgets. Religious and economic systems resort to military measures. The Nazi "solution to the Jewish problem" was a competitve struggle to the death. And in competition of that sort the strong do seem to survive. But no man survives for long, or any governmental, religious, or economic agency for very long. What *evolve* are practices.

In neither biological nor cultural evolution is competition with other forms the only important condition of selection. Both species and cultures "compete" first of all with the physical environment. Most of the anatomy and physiology of a species is concerned with breathing, feeding, maintaining a suitable temperature, surviving danger, fighting infection, procreating, and so on. Only a small part is concerned with, and hence has survived because of, success in fighting other members of the same species or other species. Similarly, most of the practices which compose a culture are concerned with sustenance and safety rather than with competition with other cultures, and they have been selected by contingencies of survival in which successful competition has played a minor role.

A culture is not the product of a creative "group mind" or the expression of a "general will." No society began with a social contract, no economic system with the idea of barter or wages, no family structure with an insight into the advantages of cohabitation. A culture evolves when new practices further the survival of those who practice them.

When it has become clear that a culture may survive or perish, some of its members may begin to act to promote its survival. To the two values which, as we have seen, may affect those in a position to make use of a technology of behavior—the personal "goods," which are reinforcing because of the human genetic endowment, and the "goods of others," which are derived from personal reinforcers—we must now add a third, the good of the culture. But why is it effective?

Why should people in the last third of the twentieth
century care about what the people in the last third
of the twenty-first century will look like, how they will
be governed, how and why they will work productively, what they will know, or what their books, pictures, and music will be like? No current reinforcers
can be derived from anything so remote. Why, then,
should a person regard the survival of his culture as a
"good"?

It is no help, of course, to say that a person acts "because he feels concern for the survival of his culture."
Feelings about any institution depend upon the reinforcers the institution uses. What a person feels about
a government may range from the most zealous patriotism to the most abject fear, depending on the nature of
the controlling practices. What a person feels about an
economic system may range from enthusiastic support
to bitter resentment, depending on the way the system
uses positive and negative reinforcers. And what a person feels about the survival of his culture will depend
on the measures used by the culture to induce its members to work for its survival. The measures explain the
support; the feelings are by-products. Nor is it any help
to say that someone suddenly gets the idea of working
for the survival of a culture and transmits it to others.
An "idea" is at least as difficult to explain as the practices said to express it, and much less accessible. But
how are we to explain the practices?

Much of what a person does to promote the survival
of a culture is not "intentional"—that is, it is not done
because it increases survival value. A culture survives
if those who carry it survive, and this depends in part
upon certain genetic susceptibilities to reinforcement,
as the result of which behavior making for survival in
a given environment is shaped and maintained. Practices which induce the individual to work for the good

of others presumably further the survival of others and hence the survival of the culture the others carry.

Institutions may derive effective reinforcers from events which will occur only after a person's death. They mediate security, justice, order, knowledge, wealth, health, and so on, only part of which the individual will enjoy. In a five-year plan or an austerity program, people are induced to work hard and forgo certain kinds of reinforcers in return for the promise of reinforcers to be received later, but many of them will not live to enjoy the deferred consequences. (Rousseau made this point with respect to education: half the children who submitted to the punitive educational practices of his time never lived to enjoy the supposed benefits.) The honors accorded the living hero outlast him as memorials. Accumulated wealth outlasts the accumulator, as does accumulated knowledge; wealthy men establish foundations under their names, and science and scholarship have their heroes. The Christian notion of life after death may have grown out of the social reinforcement of those who suffer for their religion while still alive. Heaven is portrayed as a collection of positive reinforcers and hell as a collection of negative, although they are contingent upon behavior executed *before death.* (Personal survival after death may be a metaphorical adumbration of the evolutionary concept of survival value.) The individual is not, of course, directly affected by any of these things; he simply gains from conditioned reinforcers used by other members of his culture who do outlast him and are directly affected.

None of this will explain what we might call a pure concern for the survival of a culture, but we do not really need an explanation. Just as we do not need to explain the origin of a genetic mutation in order to account for its effect in natural selection, so we do not need to explain the origin of a cultural practice in order to account for its contribution to the survival of a culture. The simple fact is that a culture which *for any reason* induces its members to work for its survival, or for the survival of some of its practices, is more likely to survive. Survival is the only value according to which a culture is eventually to be judged, and any practice that furthers survival has survival value by definition.

If it is not very satisfactory to say that any culture which induces its members to work for its survival for any reason is therefore more likely to survive and perpetuate the practice, we must remember that there is very little to explain. Cultures seldom generate a pure concern for their survival—a concern completely free from the jingoistic trappings, the racial features, the geographical locations, or the institutionalized practices with which cultures tend to be identified.

When the goods of others are challenged, especially the goods of organized others, it is not easy to answer by pointing to deferred advantages. Thus, a government is challenged when its citizens refuse to pay taxes, serve in the armed forces, participate in elections, and so on, and it may meet the challenge either by strengthening its contingencies or by bringing deferred gains to bear on the behavior at issue. But how can it answer the question: "Why should I care whether my government, or my form of government, survives long after my death?" Similarly, a religious organization is challenged when its communicants do not go to church, contribute to its support, take political action in its interests, and so on, and it may meet the challenge by strengthening its contingencies or pointing to deferred gains But what is its answer to the question: "Why should I work for the long-term survival of my religion?" An economic system is challenged when people do not work productively, and it may respond by sharpening its contingencies or pointing to deferred advantages. But what is its answer to the question: "Why should I be concerned about the survival of a particular kind of economic system?" The only honest answer to that kind of question seems to be this: "There is no good reason why you should be concerned, but if your culture has not convinced you that there is, so much the worse for your culture."

It is even more difficult to explain any action designed to strengthen a single culture for all mankind. A Pax Romana or Americana, a world made safe for democracy, world communism, or a "catholic" church commands the support of strong institutions, but a "pure" world culture does not. It is not likely to evolve from successful competition between religious, governmental, or economic agencies. We can nevertheless point to many reasons why people should now be concerned for the good of all mankind. The great problems of the world today are all global. Overpopulation, the depletion of resources, the pollution of the environment, and the possibility of a nuclear holocaust—these are the not-so-remote consequences of present courses of action. But pointing to consequences is not enough. We must arrange contingencies under which consequences have an effect. How can the cultures of the world bring these terrifying possibilities to bear on the behavior of their members?

The process of cultural evolution would not come to an end, of course, if there were only one culture, as biological evolution would not come to an end if there were only one major species—presumably man. Some important conditions of selection would be changed and others eliminated, but mutations would still occur and undergo selection, and new practices would continue to evolve. There would be no reason to speak of *a* culture. It would be clear that we were dealing only with practices, just as in a single species we should be dealing only with traits.

The evolution of a culture raises certain questions about so-called "values" which have not been fully answered. Is the evolution of a culture "progress"? What is its goal? Is the goal a kind of consequence quite different from the consequences, real or spurious, which induce individuals to work for the survival of their culture?

A structural analysis may seem to avoid these questions. If we confine ourselves simply to what people do, then a culture seems to evolve simply by passing through a sequence of stages. Though a culture may skip a stage, some kind of characteristic order may be demonstrated. The structuralist looks for an explanation of why one stage follows another in the pattern of the sequence. Technically speaking, he tries to account for a dependent variable without relating it to any independent variables. The fact that evolution occurs in time suggests, however, that time may be a useful independent variable. As Leslie White has put it: "Evolution may be defined as a temporal sequence of forms: one form grows out of another; culture advances from one stage to another. In this process time is as integral a factor as change of form."

A directed change in time is often spoken of as "development." Geologists trace the development of the earth through various eras, and paleontologists trace the development of species. Psychologists follow the development of, say, psychosexual adjustment. The development of a culture may be followed in its use of materials (from stone to bronze to iron), in its ways of getting food (from gathering to hunting and fishing to cultivation), in its use of economic power (from feudalism to commercialism to industrialism to socialism), and so on.

Facts of this sort are useful, but change occurs not because of the passage of time, but because of what happens while time is passing. The Cretaceous period in geology did not appear at a given stage in the development of the earth because of a predetermined fixed sequence but because a preceding condition of the earth led to certain changes. The horse's hoof did not develop because time passed but because certain mutations were selected when they favored survival in the environment in which the horse was living. The size of a child's vocabulary or the grammatical forms he uses are not a function of developmental age but of the verbal contingencies which have prevailed in the community to which he has been exposed. A child develops the "concept of inertia" at a given age only because of the social and nonsocial contingencies of reinforcement which have generated the behavior said to show the possession of the concept. The contingencies "develop" as much as the behavior they generate. If developmental stages follow one another in a fixed order, it is because one stage builds the conditions responsible for the next. A child must walk before he can run or jump; he must have a rudimentary vocabulary before he can "put words into grammatical patterns"; he must possess simple behaviors before he can acquire the behavior said to show the possession of "complex concepts."

The same issues arise in the development of a culture. Food-gathering practices naturally precede agriculture, not because of an essential pattern but because people must stay alive somehow (as by gathering food) until agricultural practices can be acquired. The necessary order in the historical determinism of

Karl Marx is in the contingencies. Class struggle is a crude way of representing the ways in which men control each other. The rise of the power of merchants and the decline of feudalism and the later appearance of an industrial age (possibly to be followed by socialism or a welfare state) depend largely upon changes in economic contingencies of reinforcement.

A pure developmentalism, contenting itself with patterns of sequential change in structure, misses the chance to explain behavior in terms of genetic and environmental histories. It also misses the chance to change the order in which stages succeed one another or the speed with which they do so. In a standard environment a child may acquire concepts in a standard order, but the order is determined by contingencies that may be changed. Similarly, a culture may develop through a sequence of stages as contingencies develop, but a different order of contingencies can be designed. We cannot change the age of the earth or of the child, but in the case of the child we need not wait for time to pass in order to change the things that happen in time.

The concept of development becomes entangled with so-called "values" when directed change is regarded as *growth*. A growing apple passes through a sequence of stages, and one stage is best. We reject green and rotten apples; only the ripe apple is good. By analogy we speak of a mature person and a mature culture. The farmer works to bring his crops safely to maturity, and parents, teachers, and therapists strive to produce a mature person. Changing in the direction of maturity is often valued as "becoming." If change is interrupted, we speak of arrested or fixated development, which we try to correct. When the change is slow, we speak of retardation and work for acceleration. But these highly prized values become meaningless (or worse) when maturity is reached. No one is anxious to "become" senile; the mature person would be pleased to have his development arrested or fixated; from that point on he would not mind being a retardate.

It is a mistake to suppose that all change or development is growth. The present condition of the earth's surface is not mature or immature; the horse has not, so far as we know, reached some final and presumably optimal stage in evolutionary development. If a child's language seems to grow like an embryo, it is only because the environmental contingencies have been neglected. The feral child has no language, not because his isolation has interfered with some growth process, but because he has not been exposed to a verbal community. We have no reason to call any culture mature in the sense that further growth is unlikely or that it would necessarily be a kind of deterioration. We call some cultures underdeveloped or immature in contrast with others we call "advanced," but it is a crude form of jingoism to imply that any government, religion, or economic system is mature.

The main objection to the metaphor of growth, in considering either the development of an individual or the evolution of a culture, is that it emphasizes a terminal state which does not have a function. We say that an organism grows *toward* maturity or *in order to reach maturity*. Maturity becomes a goal, and progress becomes movement toward a goal. A goal is literally a terminus—the end of something such as a foot race. It has no effect on the race except to bring it to an end. The word is used in this relatively empty sense when we say that the goal of life is death or that the goal of evolution is to fill the earth with life. Death is no doubt the end of life, and a full world may be the end of evolution, but these terminal conditions have no bearing on the processes through which they are reached. We do not live *in order to* die, and evolution does not proceed *in order to* fill the earth with life.

The goal as the end of a race is easily confused with winning, hence with the reasons for running it or the purpose of the runner. Early students of learning used mazes and other devices in which a goal seemed to show the position of a reinforcer with respect to the behavior of which it was a consequence; the organism went *toward* a goal. But the important relation is temporal, not spatial. Behavior is *followed by* reinforcement; it does not pursue and overtake it. We explain the development of a species and of the behavior of a member of the species by pointing to the selective action of contingencies of survival and contingencies of reinforcement. Both the species and the behavior of the individual develop when they are shaped and maintained by their effects on the world around them. That is the only role of the future.

But this does not mean that there is no direction. Many efforts have been made to characterize evolution as directed change—for example, as a steady increase in complexity of structure, in sensitivity to stimulation, or in the effective utilization of energy. There is another important possibility: *both kinds of evolution make organisms more sensitive to the consequences of their action.* Organisms most likely to be changed by certain kinds of consequences have presumably had an advantage, and a culture brings the individual under the control of remote consequences which could have played no part in the physical evolution of the species. A remote personal good becomes effective when a person is controlled for the good of others, and the culture which induces

Beyond Freedom and Dignity

137

some of its members to work for its survival brings an
even more remote consequence to bear.

The task of the cultural designer is to accelerate
the development of practices which bring the remote
consequences of behavior into play. We turn now to
some of the problems he faces.

* * *

The social environment is what is called a culture.
It shapes and maintains the behavior of those who
live in it. A given culture evolves as new practices
arise, possibly for irrelevant reasons, and are selected
by their contribution to the strength of the culture as
it "competes" with the physical environment and with
other cultures. A major step is the emergence of practices which induce members to work for the survival
of their culture. Such practices cannot be traced to
personal goods, even when used for the good of others,
since the survival of a culture beyond the lifetime of
the individual cannot serve as a source of conditioned
reinforcers. Other people may survive the person they
induce to act for their good, and the culture whose
survival is at issue is often identified with them or
their organizations, but the evolution of a culture
introduces an additional kind of good or value. A
culture which *for any reason* induces its members to
work for its survival is more likely to survive. It is a
matter of the good of the culture, not of the individual. Explicit design promotes that good by accelerat-
ing the evolutionary process, and since a science and
a technology of behavior make for better design, they
are important "mutations" in the evolution of a culture. If there is any purpose or direction in the
evolution of a culture, it has to do with bringing people
under the control of more and more of the consequences of their behavior.

8
The Design of
a Culture

MANY PEOPLE ARE ENGAGED in the design
and redesign of cultural practices. They make changes
in the things they use and the way they use them.
They invent better mousetraps and computers and
discover better ways of raising children, paying wages,
collecting taxes, and helping people with problems.
We need not spend much time on the word "better";
it is simply the comparative of "good," and goods are
reinforcers. One camera is called better than another
because of what happens when it is used. A manu-
facturer induces potential buyers to "value" his camera
by guaranteeing that it will perform in satisfactory
ways, by quoting what users have said about its performance, and so on. It is, of course, much harder to
call one culture better than another, in part because
more consequences need to be taken into account.

No one knows the *best* way of raising children, paying workers, maintaining law and order, teaching, or
making people creative, but it is possible to propose
better ways than we now have and to support them
by predicting and eventually demonstrating more reinforcing results. This has been done in the past with
the help of personal experience and folk wisdom, but
a scientific analysis of human behavior is obviously
relevant. It helps in two ways: it defines what is to
be done and suggests ways of doing it. How badly it

is needed is indicated by a recent discussion in a news weekly about what is wrong with America. The problem was described as "a disturbed psychic condition of the young," "a recession of the spirit," "a psychic downturn," and "a spiritual crisis," which were attributed to "anxiety," "uncertainty," "malaise," "alienation," "generalized despair," and several other moods and states of mind, all interacting in the familiar intrapsychic pattern (lack of social assurance being said to lead to alienation, for example, and frustration to aggression). Most readers probably knew what the writer was talking about and may have felt that he was saying something useful, but the passage—which is not exceptional—has two characteristic defects which explain our failure to deal adequately with cultural problems: the troublesome behavior is not actually described, and nothing that can be done to change it is mentioned.

Consider a young man whose world has suddenly changed. He has graduated from college and is going to work, let us say, or has been inducted into the armed services. Most of the behavior he has acquired up to this point proves useless in his new environment. The behavior he actually exhibits can be described, and the description translated, as follows: he lacks assurance or feels insecure or is unsure of himself (*his behavior is weak and inappropriate*); he is dissatisfied or discouraged (*he is seldom reinforced, and as a result his behavior undergoes extinction*); he is frustrated (*extinction is accompanied by emotional responses*); he feels uneasy or anxious (*his behavior frequently has unavoidable aversive consequences which have emotional effects*); there is nothing he wants to do or enjoys doing well, he has no feeling of craftsmanship, no sense of leading a purposeful life, no sense of accomplishment (*he is rarely reinforced for doing anything*); he feels guilty or ashamed (*he has previously been pun-ished for idleness or failure, which now evokes emo-tional responses*); he is disappointed in himself or disgusted with himself (*he is no longer reinforced by the admiration of others, and the extinction which fol-lows has emotional effects*); he becomes hypochon-driacal (*he concludes that he is ill*) or neurotic (*he engages in a variety of ineffective modes of escape*); and he experiences an identity crisis (*he does not recognize the person he once called "I"*).

The italicized paraphrases are too brief to be pre-cise, but they suggest the possibility of an alternative account, which alone suggests effective action. To the young man himself the important things are no doubt the various states of his body. They are salient stimuli, and he has learned to use them in traditional ways to explain his behavior to himself and others. What he tells us about his feelings may permit us to make some informed guesses about what is wrong with the con-tingencies, but we must go directly to the contingencies if we want to be sure, *and it is the contingencies which must be changed if his behavior is to be changed.*

Feelings and states of mind still dominate discus-sions of human behavior for many reasons For one thing, they have long obscured the alternatives that might replace them; it is hard to see behavior as such without reading into it many of the things it is said to express. The selective action of the environment has remained obscure because of its nature. Nothing less than an experimental analysis was needed to discover the significance of contingencies of reinforcement, and contingencies remain almost out of reach of casual observation. This is easy to demonstrate The contin-gencies arranged in an operant laboratory are often complex, but they are still simpler than many contin-gencies in the world at large. Yet one who is unfamiliar

with laboratory practice will find it hard to see what is
going on in an experimental space. He sees an organism behaving in a few simple ways, in the presence of
various stimuli that change from time to time, and he
may see an occasional reinforcing event—for example,
the appearance of food which the organism eats. The
facts are all clear, but casual observation alone will
seldom reveal the contingencies. Our observer will not
be able to explain why the organism behaves as it
does. And if he cannot understand what he sees in a
simplified laboratory environment, how can we expect
him to make sense of what is happening in daily life?

The experimenter has, of course, additional information. He knows something about the genetics of his
subject, at least to the extent that he has studied other
subjects of the same strain. He knows something about
past history—about earlier contingencies to which the
organism has been exposed, its schedule of deprivation, and so on. But our observer did not fail because
he lacked these additional facts; he failed because he
could not see what was happening before his eyes. In
an experiment on operant behavior the important data
are changes in the probability of a response, usually
observed as changes in rate, but it is difficult if not
impossible to follow a change in rate through casual
observation. We are not well equipped to see changes
taking place over fairly long periods of time. The experimenter can see such changes in his records. What
seems like rather sporadic responding may prove to be
a stage in an orderly process. The experimenter also
knows about the prevailing contingencies (he has, in
fact, constructed the apparatus that arranges them).
If our casual observer spent enough time, he might
discover some of the contingencies, but he would do so
only if he knew what to look for. Until contingencies
had been arranged and their effects studied in the

laboratory, little effort was made to find them in daily life. This is the sense in which, as we noted in Chapter 1, an experimental analysis makes possible an effective interpretation of human behavior. It permits us to neglect irrelevant details, no matter how dramatic, and to emphasize features which, without the help of the analysis, would be dismissed as trivial.

(The reader may have been inclined to dismiss frequent references to contingencies of reinforcement as a new fashion in technical jargon, but it is not simply a matter of talking about old things in new ways. Contingencies *are* ubiquitous; they cover the classical fields of intention and purpose, but in a much more useful way, and they provide alternative formulations of so-called "mental processes." Many details have never been dealt with before, and no traditional terms are available in discussing them. The full significance of the concept is no doubt still far from adequately recognized.)

Beyond interpretation lies practical action. Contingencies are accessible, and as we come to understand the relations between behavior and the environment, we discover new ways of changing behavior. The outlines of a technology are already clear. An assignment is stated as behavior to be produced or modified, and relevant contingencies are then arranged. A programmed sequence of contingencies may be needed. The technology has been most successful where behavior can be fairly easily specified and where appropriate contingencies can be constructed—for example, in child care, schools, and the management of retardates and institutionalized psychotics. The same principles are being applied, however, in the preparation of instructional materials at all educational levels, in psychotherapy beyond simple management, in rehabilitation, in industrial management, in urban design, and in many other fields of human behavior. There are many varieties of "behavior modification" and many different formulations, but they all agree on the essential point: behavior can be changed by changing the conditions of which it is a function.

Such a technology is ethically neutral. It can be used by villain or saint. There is nothing in a methodology which determines the values governing its use. We are concerned here, however, not merely with practices, but with the design of a whole culture, and the survival of a culture then emerges as a special kind of value. A person may design a better way of raising children primarily to escape from children who do not behave well. He may solve his problem, for example, by being a martinet. Or his new method may promote the good of the children or of parents in general. It may demand time and effort and the sacrifice of personal reinforcers, but he will propose and use it if he has been sufficiently induced to work for the good of others. If he is strongly reinforced when he sees other people enjoying themselves, for example, he will design an environment in which children are happy. If his culture has induced him to take an interest in its survival, however, he may study the contribution which people make to their culture as a result of their early history, and he may design a better method in order to increase that contribution. Those who adopt the method may suffer some loss in personal reinforcers.

The same three kinds of values may be detected in the design of other cultural practices. The classroom teacher may devise new ways of teaching which make life easier for him, or which please his students (who in turn reinforce him), or which make it likely that his students will contribute as much as possible to their culture. The industrialist may design a wage sys-

tem that maximizes his profits, or works for the good
of his employees, or most effectively produces the goods
a culture needs, with a minimal consumption of resources and minimal pollution. A party in power may
act primarily to keep its power, or to reinforce those it
governs (who in return keep it in power), or to promote the state, as by instituting a program of austerity
which may cost the party both power and support.

The same three levels may be detected in the design
of a culture as a whole. If the designer is an individualist, he will design a world in which he will be under
minimal aversive control and will accept his own goods
as the ultimate values. If he has been exposed to an
appropriate social environment, he will design for the
good of others, possibly with a loss of personal goods.
If he is concerned primarily with survival value, he
will design a culture with an eye to whether it will
work.

When a culture induces some of its members to work
for its survival, what are they to do? They will need
to foresee some of the difficulties the culture will en-
counter. These usually lie far in the future, and details
are not always clear. Apocalyptic visions have had a
long history, but only recently has much attention been
paid to the prediction of the future. There is nothing
to be done about completely unpredictable difficulties,
but we may foresee some trouble by extrapolating current trends. It may be enough simply to observe a
steady increase in the number of people on the earth,
in the size and location of nuclear stockpiles, or in the
pollution of the environment and the depletion of
natural resources; we may then change practices to
induce people to have fewer children, spend less on
nuclear weapons, stop polluting the environment, and
consume resources at a lower rate, respectively.

We do not need to predict the future to see some of the ways in which the strength of a culture depends upon the behavior of its members. A culture that maintains civil order and defends itself against attack frees its members from certain kinds of threats and presumably provides more time and energy for other things (particularly if order and security are not maintained by force). A culture needs various goods for its survival, and its strength must depend in part on the economic contingencies which maintain enterprising and productive labor, on the availability of the tools of production, and on the development and conservation of resources. A culture is presumably stronger if it induces its members to maintain a safe and healthful environment, to provide medical care, and to maintain a population density appropriate to its resources and space. A culture must be transmitted from generation to generation, and its strength will presumably depend on what and how much its new members learn, either through informal instructional contingencies or in educational institutions. A culture needs the support of its members, and it must provide for the pursuit and achievement of happiness if it is to prevent disaffection or defection. A culture must be reasonably stable, but it must also change, and it will presumably be strongest if it can avoid excessive respect for tradition and fear of novelty on the one hand and excessively rapid change on the other. Lastly, a culture will have a special measure of survival value if it encourages its members to examine its practices and to experiment with new ones.

A culture is very much like the experimental space used in the analysis of behavior. Both are sets of contingencies of reinforcement. A child is born into a culture as an organism is placed in an experimental space. Designing a culture is like designing an experiment;

contingencies are arranged and effects noted. In an experiment we are interested in what happens, in designing a culture with whether it will work. This is the difference between science and technology.

A collection of cultural designs is to be found in the utopian literature. Writers have described their versions of the good life and suggested ways of achieving them. Plato, in *The Republic,* chose a political solution; Saint Augustine, in *The City of God,* a religious one. Thomas More and Francis Bacon, both lawyers, turned to law and order, and the Rousseauean utopists of the eighteenth century, to a supposed natural goodness in man. The nineteenth century looked for economic solutions, and the twentieth century saw the rise of what may be called behavioral utopias in which a full range of social contingencies began to be discussed (often satirically).

Utopian writers have been at pains to simplify their assignment. A utopian community is usually composed of a relatively small number of people living together in one place and in stable contact with each other. They can practice an informal ethical control and minimize the role of organized agencies. They can learn from each other rather than from the specialists called teachers. They can be kept from behaving badly toward each other through censure rather than the specialized punishments of a legal system. They can produce and exchange goods without specifying values in terms of money. They can help those who have become ill, infirm, disturbed, or aged with a minimum of institutional care. Troublesome contacts with other cultures are avoided through geographical isolation (utopias tend to be located on islands or surrounded by high mountains), and the transition to a new culture is facilitated by some formalized break with the past, such as a ritual of rebirth (utopias are often set in the distant future so that the necessary evolution of the culture seems plausible). A utopia is a total social environment, and all its parts work together. The home does not conflict with the school or the street, religion does not conflict with government, and so on.

Perhaps the most important feature of the utopian design, however, is that the survival of a community can be made important to its members. The small size, the isolation, the internal coherence—all these give a community an identity which makes its success or failure conspicuous. The fundamental question in all utopias is "Would it really work?" The literature is worth considering just because it emphasizes experimentation. A traditional culture has been examined and found wanting, and a new version has been set up to be tested and redesigned as circumstances dictate.

The simplification in utopian writing, which is nothing more than the simplification characteristic of science, is seldom feasible in the world at large, and there are many other reasons why it is difficult to put an explicit design into effect. A large fluid population cannot be brought under informal social or ethical control because social reinforcers like praise and blame are not exchangeable for the personal reinforcers on which they are based. Why should anyone be affected by the praise or blame of someone he will never see again? Ethical control may survive in small groups, but the control of the population as a whole must be delegated to specialists—to police, priests, owners, teachers, therapists, and so on, with their specialized reinforcers and their codified contingencies. These are probably already in conflict with each other and will almost certainly be in conflict with any new set of contingencies. Where it is not too difficult to change informal instruction, for example, it is nearly impossible to change an educational establishment. It is fairly easy to change marriage, divorce, and child-bearing practices as the significance for the culture changes but nearly impossible to change the religious principles which dictate such practices. It is easy to change the extent to which various kinds of behavior are accepted as right but difficult to change the laws of a government. The reinforcing values of goods are more flexible than the values set by economic agencies. The word of authority is more unyielding than the facts of which it speaks.

It is not surprising that, so far as the real world is concerned, the word utopian means unworkable. History seems to offer support; various utopian designs have been proposed for nearly twenty-five hundred years, and most attempts to set them up have been ignominious failures. But historical evidence is always against the probability of anything new; that is what is meant by history. Scientific discoveries and inventions are improbable; that is what is meant by discovery and invention. And if planned economies, benevolent dictatorships, perfectionistic societies, and other utopian ventures have failed, we must remember that unplanned, undictated, and unperfected cultures have failed too. A failure is not always a mistake; it may simply be the best one can do under the circumstances. The real mistake is to stop trying. Perhaps we cannot now design a successful culture as a whole, but we can design better practices in a piecemeal fashion. The behavioral processes in the world at large are the same as those in a utopian community, and practices have the same effects for the same reasons.

The same advantages are also to be found in emphasizing contingencies of reinforcement in lieu of states of mind or feelings. It is no doubt a serious problem, for example, that students no longer respond in traditional ways to educational environments; they drop out of school, possibly for long periods of time, they take only courses which they enjoy or which seem to have relevance to their problems, they destroy school property and attack teachers and officials. But we shall not solve this problem by "cultivating on the part of our public a respect it does not now have for scholarship as such and for the practicing scholar and teacher." (The cultivation of respect is a metaphor in the horticultural tradition.) What is wrong is the educational environment. We need to design contingencies under which students acquire behavior useful to them and their culture—contingencies that do not have troublesome by-products and that generate the behavior said to "show respect for learning." It is not difficult to see what is wrong in most educational environments, and much has already been done to design materials which make learning as easy as possible and to construct contingencies, in the classroom and elsewhere, which give students powerful reasons for getting an education.

A serious problem also arises when young people refuse to serve in the armed forces and desert or defect to other countries, but we shall not make an appreciable change by "inspiring greater loyalty or patriotism." What must be changed are the contingencies which induce young people to behave in given ways toward their governments. Governmental sanctions remain almost entirely punitive, and the unfortunate by-products are sufficiently indicated by the extent of domestic disorder and international conflict. It is a serious problem that we remain almost continuously at war with other nations, but we shall not get far by attacking "the tensions which lead to war," or by appeasing warlike spirits, or by changing the minds of men (in which, UNESCO tells us, wars begin). What must be changed are the circumstances under which men and nations make war.

We may also be disturbed by the fact that many young people work as little as possible, or that workers are not very productive and often absent, or that products are often of poor quality, but we shall not get far by inspiring a "sense of craftsmanship or pride in one's work," or a "sense of the dignity of labor," or, where crafts and skills are a part of the caste mores, by changing "the deep emotional resistance of the caste superego," as one writer has put it. Something is wrong with the contingencies which induce men to work industriously and carefully. (Other kinds of economic contingencies are wrong too.)

Walter Lippmann has said that "the supreme question before mankind" is how men can save themselves from the catastrophe which threatens them, but to answer it we must do more than discover how men can "make themselves willing and able to save themselves." We must look to the contingencies that induce people to act to increase the chances that their cultures will survive. We have the physical, biological, and behavioral technologies needed "to save ourselves"; the problem is how to get people to use them. It may be that "utopia has only to be willed," but what does that mean? What are the principal specifications of a culture that will survive because it induces its members to work for its survival?

The application of a science of behavior to the design of a culture is an ambitious proposal, often thought to be utopian in the pejorative sense, and some reasons for skepticism deserve comment. It is often asserted, for example, that there are fundamental differences between the real world and the laboratory in which behavior is analyzed. Where the laboratory setting is contrived, the real world is natural; where the setting is simple, the world is complex; where processes observed in the laboratory reveal order, behavior else-where is characteristically confused. These are real differences, but they may not remain so as a science of behavior advances, and they are often not to be taken seriously even now.

The difference between contrived and natural con-ditions is not a serious one. It may be natural for a pigeon to flick leaves about and find bits of food be-neath some of them, in the sense that the contingencies are standard parts of the environment in which the pigeon evolved. The contingencies under which a pigeon pecks an illuminated disk on a wall and food then appears in a dispenser below the disk are clearly unnatural. But although the programming equipment in the laboratory is contrived and the arrangement of leaves and seeds natural, the schedules according to which behavior is reinforced can be made identical. The natural schedule is the "variable-ratio" schedule of the laboratory, and we have no reason to doubt that behavior is affected by it in the same way under both conditions. When the effects of the schedule are studied with programming equipment we begin to understand the behavior observed in nature, and as more and more complex contingencies of reinforcement have come to be investigated in the laboratory, more and more light has been thrown on the natural contingencies.

And so with simplification. Every experimental sci-ence simplifies the conditions under which it works, particularly in the early stages of an investigation. An analysis of behavior naturally begins with simple or-ganisms behaving in simple ways in simple settings. When a reasonable degree of orderliness appears, the arrangements can be made more complex. We move forward only as rapidly as our successes permit, and progress often does not seem rapid enough. Behavior is a discouraging field because we are in such close contact with it. Early physicists, chemists, and biologists enjoyed a kind of natural protection against the complexity of their fields; they were untouched by vast ranges of relevant facts. They could select a few things for study and dismiss the rest of nature either as irrelevant or as obviously out of reach. If Gilbert or Faraday or Maxwell had had even a quick glimpse of what is now known about electricity, they would have had much more trouble in finding starting points and in formulating principles which did not seem "oversimplified." Fortunately for them, much of what is now known in their fields came to be known as the result of research and its technological uses, and it did not need to be considered until formulations were well advanced. The behavioral scientist has had no such luck. He is all too aware of his own behavior as part of his subject matter. Subtle perceptions, tricks of memory, the vagaries of dreams, the apparently intuitive solutions of problems—these and many other things about human behavior insistently demand attention. It is much more difficult to find a starting point and to arrive at formulations which do not seem too simple.

The interpretation of the complex world of human affairs in terms of an experimental analysis is no doubt often oversimplified. Claims have been exaggerated and limitations neglected. But the really great oversimplification is the traditional appeal to states of mind, feelings, and other aspects of the autonomous man which a behavioral analysis is replacing. The ease with which mentalistic explanations can be invented on the spot is perhaps the best gauge of how little attention we should pay to them. And the same may be said for traditional practices. The technology which has emerged from an experimental analysis should be evaluated only in comparison with what is done in other ways. What, after all, have we to show for non-scientific or prescientific good judgment, or common sense, or the insights gained through personal experience? It is science or nothing, and the only solution to simplification is to learn how to deal with complexities.

A science of behavior is not yet ready to solve all our problems, but it is a science in progress, and its ultimate adequacy cannot now be judged. When critics assert that it cannot account for this or that aspect of human behavior, they usually imply that it will never be able to do so, but the analysis continues to develop and is in fact much further advanced than its critics usually realize.

The important thing is not so much to know how to solve a problem as to know how to look for a solution. The scientists who approached President Roosevelt with a proposal to build a bomb so powerful that it could end the Second World War within a few days could not say that they knew how to build it. All they could say was that they knew how to go about finding out. The behavioral problems to be solved in the world today are no doubt more complex than the practical use of nuclear fission, and the basic science by no means as far advanced, but we know where to start looking for solutions.

A proposal to design a culture with the help of a scientific analysis often leads to Cassandran prophecies of disaster. The culture will not work as planned, and unforeseen consequences may be catastrophic. Proof is seldom offered, possibly because history seems to be on the side of failure: many plans have gone wrong, and possibly just because they were planned. The threat in a designed culture, said Mr. Krutch, is that the unplanned "may never erupt again." But it is hard to justify the trust which is placed in accident. It is true that accidents have been responsible for almost everything men have achieved to date, and they will no doubt continue to contribute to human accomplishments, but there is no virtue in an accident as such. The unplanned also goes wrong. The idiosyncrasies of a jealous ruler who regards any disturbance as an offense against him may have an accidental survival value if law and order are maintained, but the military strategies of a paranoid leader are of the same provenance and may have an entirely different effect. The industry which arises in the unrestrained pursuit of happiness may have an accidental survival value when war matériel is suddenly needed, but it may also exhaust natural resources and pollute the environment.

If a planned culture necessarily meant uniformity or regimentation, it might indeed work against further evolution. If men were very much alike, they would be less likely to hit upon or design new practices, and a culture which made people as much alike as possible might slip into a standard pattern from which there would be no escape. That would be bad design, but if we are looking for variety, we should not fall back upon accident. Many accidental cultures have been marked by uniformity and regimentation. The exigencies of administration in governmental, religious, and economic systems breed uniformity, because it simplifies the problem of control. Traditional educational establishments specify what the student is to learn at what age and administer tests to make sure that the specifications are met. The codes of governments and religions are usually quite explicit and allow little room for diversity or change. The only hope is *planned* diversification, in which the importance of variety is recognized. The breeding of plants and animals moves toward uniformity when uniformity is important (as in simplifying agriculture or animal husbandry), but it also requires planned diversity.

Planning does not prevent useful accidents. For many thousands of years people used fibers (such as cotton, wool, or silk) from sources which were accidental in the sense that they were the products of contingencies of survival not closely related to the contingencies which made them useful to men. Synthetic fibers, on the other hand, are explicitly designed; their usefulness is taken into account. But the production of synthetic fibers does not make the evolution of a new kind of cotton, wool, or silk any the less likely. Accidents still occur, and indeed, are furthered by those investigating new possibilities. It might be said that science maximizes accidents. The physicist does not confine himself to the temperatures which occur accidentally in the world at large, he produces a continuous series of temperatures over a very wide range. The behavioral scientist does not confine himself to the schedules of reinforcement which happen to occur in nature, he constructs a great variety of schedules, some of which might never arise by accident. There is no virtue in the accidental nature of an accident. A culture evolves as new practices appear and undergo selection, and we cannot wait for them to turn up by chance.

Another kind of opposition to a new cultural design can be put this way: "I wouldn't like it," or in translation, "The culture would be aversive and would not reinforce me in the manner to which I am accustomed." The word reform is in bad odor, for it is usually associated with the destruction of reinforcers—"the Puritans have cut down the maypoles and the hobbyhorse is forgot"—but the design of a new culture is necessarily a kind of re-form, and it almost necessarily means a change of reinforcers. To eliminate a threat, for example, is to eliminate the thrill of escape; in a better world no one will "pluck this flower, safety . . . out of this nettle, danger." The reinforcing value of rest, relaxation, and leisure is necessarily weakened as labor is made less compulsive. A world in which there is no need for moral struggle will offer none of the reinforcement of a successful outcome. No convert to a religion will enjoy Cardinal Newman's release from "the stress of a great anxiety." Art and literature will no longer be based on such contingencies. We shall not only have no reason to admire people who endure suffering, face danger, or struggle to be good, it is possible that we shall have little interest in pictures or books about them. The art and literature of a new culture will be about other things.

These are prodigious changes, and we naturally give them careful consideration. The problem is to design a world which will be liked not by people as they now are but by those who live in it. "I wouldn't like it" is the complaint of the individualist who puts forth his own susceptibilities to reinforcement as established values. A world that would be liked by contemporary people would perpetuate the status quo. It would be liked because people have been taught to like it, and for reasons which do not always bear scrutiny. A better world will be liked by those who live in it because it has been designed with an eye to what is, or can be, most reinforcing.

A complete break with the past is impossible. The designer of a new culture will always be culture-bound, since he will not be able to free himself entirely from the predispositions which have been engendered by the social environment in which he has lived. To some extent he will necessarily design a world *he* likes. Moreover, a new culture must appeal to those who are to move into it, and they are necessarily the products of an older culture. Within these practical limits, however, it should be possible to minimize the effect of accidental features of prevailing cultures and to turn to the sources of the things people call good. The ultimate sources are to be found in the evolution of the species and the evolution of the culture.

It is sometimes said that the scientific design of a culture is impossible because man will simply not accept the fact that he can be controlled. Even if it could be proved that human behavior is fully determined, said Dostoevsky, a man "would still do something out of sheer perversity—he would create destruction and chaos —just to gain his point. . . . And if all this could in turn be analyzed and prevented by predicting that it would occur, then man would deliberately go mad to prove his point." The implication is that he would then be out of control, as if madness were a special kind of freedom or as if the behavior of a psychotic could not be predicted or controlled.

There is a sense in which Dostoevsky may be right. A literature of freedom may inspire a sufficiently fanatical opposition to controlling practices to generate a neurotic if not psychotic response. There are signs of emotional instability in those who have been deeply affected by the literature. We have no better indication of the plight of the traditional libertarian than the bitterness with which he discusses the possibility of a science and technology of behavior and their use in the intentional design of a culture. Name-calling is common. Arthur Koestler has referred to behaviorism as "a monumental triviality." It represents, he says, "question-begging on a heroic scale." It has spun psychology into "a modern version of the Dark Ages." Behaviorists use "pedantic jargon," and reinforcement is "an ugly word." The equipment in the operant laboratory is a "contraption." Peter Gay, whose scholarly work on the

eighteenth-century Enlightenment should have prepared him for a modern interest in cultural design, has
spoken of the "innate naïveté, intellectual bankruptcy,
and half-deliberate cruelty of behaviorism."

Another symptom is a kind of blindness to the current state of the science. Koestler has said that "the
most impressive experiment in the 'prediction and control of behavior' is to train pigeons, by operant conditioning, to strut about with their heads held unnatu-
rally high." He paraphrases "learning theory" in the
following way: "According to the Behaviorist doctrine,
all learning occurs by the hit-and-miss or trial-and-
error method. The correct response to a given stimulus
is hit upon by chance and has a rewarding or, as the
jargon has it, reinforcing effect; if the reinforcement is
strong or repeated often enough, the response will be
'stamped in' and an S-R bond, a stimulus and response
link, is formed." The paraphrase is approximately
seventy years out of date.

Other common misrepresentations include the asser-
tions that a scientific analysis treats all behavior as
responses to stimuli or as "all a matter of conditioned
reflexes," that it acknowledges no contribution to behavior from genetic endowment, and that it ignores
consciousness. (We shall see in the next chapter that
behaviorists have been responsible for the most vigorous discussion of the nature and use of what is called
consciousness.) Statements of this kind commonly appear in the humanities, a field once distinguished for
its scholarship, but it will be difficult for the historian
of the future to reconstruct current behavioral science
and technology from what is written by its critics.

Another practice is to blame behaviorism for all our
ills. The practice has a long history; the Romans blamed
the Christians, and the Christians the Romans, for
earthquakes and pestilence. Perhaps no one has gone

quite as far in blaming a scientific conception of man for the serious problems which confront us today as an anonymous writer in the London *Times Literary Supplement*:

During the last half-century our various intellectual leaders have conditioned us (the very word is a product of behaviorism) to regard the world in quantitative and covertly deterministic terms. Philosophers and psychologists alike have eroded all our old assumptions of free will and moral responsibility. The sole reality, we have been taught to believe, lies in the physical order of things. We do not initiate action; we react to a series of external stimuli. It is only in recent years that we have begun to see where this view of the world is taking us: the grim events in Dallas and Los Angeles . . .

In other words, the scientific analysis of human behavior was responsible for the assassinations of John and Robert Kennedy. A delusion of this magnitude seems to confirm Dostoevsky's prediction. Political assassination has had too long a history to have been inspired by a science of behavior. If any theory is to be blamed, it is the all but universal theory of a free and worthy autonomous man.

There are, of course, good reasons why the control of human behavior is resisted. The commonest techniques are aversive, and some sort of countercontrol is to be expected. The controllee may move out of range (the controller will work to keep him from doing so), or he may attack, and ways of doing so have emerged as important steps in the evolution of cultures. Thus, the members of a group establish the principle that it is wrong to use force and punish those who do so with any available means. Governments codify the principle and call the use of force illegal, and religions call it sinful, and both arrange contingencies to suppress it. When controllers then turn to methods which are nonaversive but have deferred aversive consequences, additional principles emerge. The group calls it wrong to control through deception, for example, and governmental and religious sanctions follow.

We have seen that the literatures of freedom and dignity have extended these countercontrolling measures in an effort to suppress all controlling practices even when they have no aversive consequences or have offsetting reinforcing consequences. The designer of a culture comes under fire because explicit design implies control (if only the control exerted by the designer). The issue is often formulated by asking: Who is to control? And the question is usually raised as if the answer were necessarily threatening. To prevent the misuse of controlling power, however, we must look not at the controller himself but at the contingencies under which he engages in control.

We are misled by differences in the conspicuousness of controlling measures. The Egyptian slave, cutting stone in a quarry for a pyramid, worked under the supervision of a soldier with a whip, who was paid to wield the whip by a paymaster, who was paid in turn by a Pharaoh, who had been convinced of the necessity of an inviolable tomb by priests, who argued to this effect because of the sacerdotal privileges and power which then came to them, and so on. A whip is a more obvious instrument of control than wages, and wages are more conspicuous than sacerdotal privileges, and privileges are more obvious than the prospect of an affluent future life. There are related differences in the results. The slave will escape if he can, the soldier or paymaster will resign or strike if the economic contingencies are too weak, the Pharaoh will dismiss his priests and start a new religion if his treasury is unduly strained, and the priests will shift their support to a rival. We are likely to single out the conspicuous exam-

ples of control, because in their abruptness and clarity
of effect, they seem to start something, but it is a great
mistake to ignore the inconspicuous forms.

The relation between the controller and the controlled is reciprocal. The scientist in the laboratory,
studying the behavior of a pigeon, designs contingencies and observes their effects. His apparatus exerts
a conspicuous control on the pigeon, but we must not
overlook the control exerted by the pigeon. The behavior of the pigeon has determined the design of the
apparatus and the procedures in which it is used. Some
such reciprocal control is characteristic of all science.
As Francis Bacon put it, nature to be commanded must
be obeyed. The scientist who designs a cyclotron is
under the control of the particles he is studying. The
behavior with which a parent controls his child, either
aversively or through positive reinforcement, is shaped
and maintained by the child's responses. A psychotherapist changes the behavior of his patient in ways
which have been shaped and maintained by his success
in changing that behavior. A government or religion
prescribes and imposes sanctions selected by their
effectiveness in controlling citizen or communicant.
An employer induces his employees to work industriously and carefully with wage systems determined by
their effects on behavior. The classroom practices of
the teacher are shaped and maintained by the effects
on his students. In a very real sense, then, the slave
controls the slave driver, the child the parent, the
patient the therapist, the citizen the government, the
communicant the priest, the employee the employer,
and the student the teacher.

It is true that the physicist designs a cyclotron *in
order to* control the behavior of certain subatomic
particles; the particles do not behave in characteristic
ways *in order to* get him to do so. The slave driver

uses a whip *in order to* make the slave work; the slave
does not work *in order to* induce the slave driver to
use a whip. The intention or purpose implied by the
phrase "in order to" is a matter of the extent to which
consequences are effective in altering behavior, and
hence the extent to which they must be taken into
account to explain it. The particle is not affected by
the consequences of its action, and there is no reason
to speak of its intention or purpose, but the slave may
be affected by the consequences of his action. Reciprocal control is not necessarily intentional in either
direction, but it becomes so when the consequences
make themselves felt. A mother learns to take up and
carry a baby in order to get it to stop crying, and she
may learn to do so before the baby learns to cry in
order to be taken up and carried. For a time only the
mother's behavior is intentional, but the baby's may
become so.

The archetypal pattern of control for the good of the
controllee is the benevolent dictator, but it is no explanation to say that he acts benevolently because he
feels benevolent, and we naturally remain suspicious
until we can point to contingencies which generate
benevolent behavior. Feelings of benevolence or compassion may accompany that behavior, but they may
also arise from irrelevant conditions. They are therefore no guarantee that a controller will necessarily
control well with respect to either himself or others
because he feels compassionate. It is said that Ramakrishna, walking with a wealthy friend, was shocked
by the poverty of some villagers. He exclaimed to his
friend, "Give these people one piece of cloth and one
good meal each, and some oil for their heads." When
his friend at first refused, Ramakrishna shed tears.
"You wretch," he cried, ". . . I'm staying with these

people. They have no one to care for them. I won't leave them." We note that Ramakrishna was concerned not with the spiritual condition of the villagers but with clothing, food, and protection against the sun. But his feelings were not a by-product of effective action; with all the power of his samadhi he had nothing to offer but compassion. Although cultures are improved by people whose wisdom and compassion may supply clues to what they do or will do, the ultimate improvement comes from the environment which makes them wise and compassionate.

The great problem is to arrange effective countercontrol and hence to bring some important consequences to bear on the behavior of the controller. Some classical examples of a lack of balance between control and countercontrol arise when control is delegated and countercontrol then becomes ineffective. Hospitals for psychotics and homes for retardates, orphans, and old people are noted for weak countercontrol, because those who are concerned for the welfare of such people often do not know what is happening. Prisons offer little opportunity for countercontrol, as the commonest controlling measures indicate. Control and countercontrol tend to become dislocated when control is taken over by organized agencies. Informal contingencies are subject to quick adjustments as their effects change, but the contingencies which organizations leave to specialists may be untouched by many of the consequences. Those who pay for education, for example, may lose touch with what is taught and with the methods used. The teacher is subject only to the countercontrol exerted by the student. As a result, a school may become wholly autocratic or wholly anarchistic, and what is taught may go out of date as the world changes or be reduced to the things students will consent to study.

There is a similar problem in jurisprudence when laws continue to be enforced which are no longer appropriate to the practices of the community. Rules never generate behavior exactly appropriate to the contingencies from which they are derived, and the discrepancy grows worse if the contingencies change while the rules remain inviolate. Similarly, the values imposed on goods by economic enterprises may lose their correspondence with the reinforcing effects of the goods, as the latter change. In short, an organized agency which is insensitive to the consequences of its practices is not subject to important kinds of countercontrol.

Self-government often seems to solve the problem by identifying the controller with the controlled. The principle of making the controller a member of the group he controls should apply to the designer of a culture. A person who designs a piece of equipment for his own use presumably takes the interests of the user into account, and the person who designs a social environment in which he is to live will presumably do the same. He will select goods or values which are important to him and arrange the kind of contingencies to which he can adapt. In a democracy the controller is found among the controlled, although he behaves in different ways in the two roles. We shall see later that there is a sense in which a culture controls itself, as a person controls himself, but the process calls for careful analysis.

The intentional design of a culture, with the implication that behavior is to be controlled, is sometimes called ethically or morally wrong. Ethics and morals are particularly concerned with bringing the remoter consequences of behavior into play. There is a morality of natural consequences. How is a person to keep from eating delicious food if it will later make him sick? Or how is he to submit to pain or exhaustion if he must do so to reach safety? Social contingencies are much more likely to raise moral and ethical issues. (As we have noted, the terms refer to the customs of groups.) How is a person to refrain from taking goods which belong to others in order to avoid the punishment which may then follow? Or how is he to submit to pain or exhaustion to gain their approval?

The practical question, which we have already considered, is how remote consequences can be made effective. Without help a person acquires very little moral or ethical behavior under either natural or social contingencies. The group supplies supporting contingencies when it describes its practices in codes or rules which tell the individual how to behave and when it enforces those rules with supplementary contingencies. Maxims, proverbs, and other forms of folk wisdom give a person reasons for obeying rules. Governments and religions formulate the contingencies they maintain somewhat more explicitly, and education imparts rules which make it possible to satisfy both natural and social contingencies without being directly exposed to them.

This is all part of the social environment called a culture, and the main effect, as we have seen, is to bring the individual under the control of the remoter consequences of his behavior. The effect has had survival value in the process of cultural evolution, since practices evolve because those who practice them are as a result better off. There is a kind of natural morality in both biological and cultural evolution. Biological evolution has made the human species more sensitive to its environment and more skillful in dealing with it. Cultural evolution was made possible by biological evolution, and it has brought the human organism under a much more sweeping control of the environment.

We say that there is something "morally wrong" about a totalitarian state, a gambling enterprise, uncontrolled piecework wages, the sale of harmful drugs, or undue personal influence, not because of any absolute set of values, but because all these things have aversive consequences. The consequences are deferred, and a science that clarifies their relation to behavior is in the best possible position to specify a better world in an ethical or moral sense. It is not true, therefore, that the empirical scientist must deny that there can be "any scientific concern with human and political values and goals," or that morality, justice, and order under law lie "beyond survival."

A special value in scientific practice is also relevant. The scientist works under contingencies that minimize immediate personal reinforcers. No scientist is "pure," in the sense of being out of reach of immediate reinforcers, but other consequences of his behavior play an important role. If he designs an experiment in a particular way, or stops an experiment at a particular point, because the result will then confirm a theory bearing his name, or will have industrial uses from which he will profit, or will impress the agencies that support his research, he will almost certainly run into trouble. The published results of scientists are subject to rapid check by others, and the scientist who allows himself to be swayed by consequences that are not part of his subject matter is likely to find himself in difficulties. To say that scientists are therefore more moral or ethical than other people, or that they have a more finely developed ethical sense, is to make the mistake of attributing to the scientist what is actually a feature of the environment in which he works.

Almost everyone makes ethical and moral judgments but this does not mean that the human species has "an inborn need or demand for ethical standards." (We could say as well that it has an inborn need or demand for unethical behavior, since almost everyone behaves unethically at some time or other.) Man has not evolved as an ethical or moral animal. He has evolved to the point at which he has constructed an ethical or moral culture. He differs from the other animals not in possessing a moral or ethical sense but in having been able to generate a moral or ethical social environment.

The intentional design of a culture and the control of human behavior it implies are essential if the human species is to continue to develop. Neither biological nor cultural evolution is any guarantee that we are inevitably moving toward a better world. Darwin concluded the *Origin of Species* with a famous sentence: "And as natural selection works solely by and for the good of each being, all corporeal and mental environments will tend to progress towards perfection." And Herbert Spencer argued that "the ultimate development of the ideal man is logically certain" (though Medawar has pointed out that Spencer changed his mind when thermodynamics suggested a different kind of terminus in the concept of entropy). Tennyson shared the eschatological optimism of his day in pointing to that "one far off divine event toward which the whole creation moves." But extinct species and extinct cultures testify to the possibility of miscarriage.

Survival value changes as conditions change. For example, a strong susceptibility to reinforcement by certain kinds of foods, sexual contact, and aggressive damage was once extremely important. When a person spent a good part of each day in searching for

food, it was important that he quickly learn where
to find it or how to catch it, but with the advent of
agriculture and animal husbandry and ways of stor-
ing food, the advantage was lost, and the capacity to
be reinforced by food now leads to overeating and
illness. When famine and pestilence frequently deci-
mated the population, it was important that men
should breed at every opportunity, but with improved
sanitation, medicine, and agriculture, the susceptibility to sexual reinforcement now means overpopulation. At a time when a person had to defend himself
against predators, including other people, it was important that any sign of damage to a predator should
reinforce the behavior having that effect, but with
the evolution of organized society the susceptibility
to that kind of reinforcement has become less important and may now interfere with more useful social
relations. It is one of the functions of a culture to
correct for these innate dispositions through the design
of techniques of control, and particularly of self-control, which moderate the effects of reinforcement.

Even under stable conditions a species may acquire
nonadaptive or maladaptive features. The process of
operant conditioning itself supplies an example. A
quick response to reinforcement must have had survival value, and many species have reached the point
at which a single reinforcement has a substantial
effect. But the more rapidly an organism learns, the
more vulnerable it is to adventitious contingencies.
The accidental appearance of a reinforcer strengthens
any behavior in progress and brings it under the
control of current stimuli. We call the result super-
stitious. So far as we know, any species capable of
learning from a few reinforcements is subject to superstition, and the consequences are often disastrous. A
culture corrects for this defect when it devises statis-

tical procedures which offset the effects of adventitious contingencies and bring behavior under the control of only those consequences which are functionally related to it.

What is needed is more "intentional" control, not less, and this is an important engineering problem. The good of a culture cannot function as the source of genuine reinforcers for the individual, and the reinforcers contrived by cultures to induce their members to work for their survival are often in conflict with personal reinforcers. The number of people explicitly engaged in improving the design of automobiles, for example, must greatly exceed the number of those concerned with improving life in city ghettos. It is not that the automobile is more important than a way of life, but rather that the economic contingencies which induce people to improve automobiles are very powerful. They arise from the personal reinforcers of those who manufacture automobiles. No reinforcers of comparable strength encourage the engineering of the pure survival of a culture. The technology of the automobile industry is also, of course, much further advanced than a technology of behavior. These facts simply underline the importance of the threat posed by the literatures of freedom and dignity.

A sensitive test of the extent to which a culture promotes its own future is its treatment of leisure. Some people have enough power to force or induce others to work for them in such a way that they themselves have little to do. They are "at leisure." So are those who live in especially beneficent climates. And so are children, the retarded or mentally ill, the aged, and others who are in the care of other people. And so are members of both affluent and welfare societies. All such people appear to be able to "do as they please," and this is a natural goal of the libertarian. Leisure is the epitome of freedom.

The species is prepared for short periods of leisure; when completely satiated by a large meal, or when danger has been successfully avoided, people relax or sleep, as other species do. If the condition survives a little longer, they may engage in various forms of play—serious behavior having at the moment non-serious consequences. But the result is very different when there is nothing to do for long periods of time. The caged lion in the zoo, well fed and safe, does not behave like the satiated lion in the field. Like the institutionalized human being, it faces the problem of leisure in its worse form: it has nothing to do. Leisure is a condition for which the human species has been badly prepared, because until very recently it was enjoyed by only a few, who contributed very little to the gene pool. Large numbers of people are now at leisure for appreciable periods of time, but there has been no chance for effective selection of either a relevant genetic endowment or a relevant culture.

When strong reinforcers are no longer effective, lesser reinforcers take over. Sexual reinforcement survives affluence or welfare because it is concerned with the survival of the species rather than the individual, and the achievement of sexual reinforcement is not a thing one delegates to others. Sexual behavior, therefore, takes a prominent place in leisure. Reinforcements which remain effective may be contrived or discovered, such as foods which continue to reinforce even when one is not hungry, drugs like alcohol, marijuana, or heroin, which happen to be reinforcing for irrelevant reasons, or massage. Any weak reinforcer becomes powerful when properly scheduled, and the variable-ratio schedule to be found in all gambling enterprises comes into its own during leisure. The same schedule explains the dedication of the hunter, fisherman, or collector, where what is caught or collected is not of any great significance. In games and sports, contingencies are especially contrived to make trivial events highly important. People at leisure also become spectators, watching the serious behavior of others, as in the Roman circus or a modern football game, or in the theater or movies, or they listen to or read accounts of the serious behavior of other people, as in gossip or literature. Little of this behavior contributes to personal survival or the survival of a culture.

Leisure has long been associated with artistic, literary, and scientific productivity. One must be at leisure to engage in these activities, and only a reasonably affluent society can support them on a broad scale. But leisure itself does not necessarily lead to art, literature, or science. Special cultural conditions are needed. Those who are concerned with the survival of their culture will therefore look closely at the contingencies which remain when the exigent contingencies in daily life have been attenuated.

It is often said that an affluent culture can afford leisure, but we cannot be sure. It is easy for those who work hard to confuse a state of leisure with reinforcement, partly because it often accompanies reinforcement, and happiness, like freedom, has long been associated with doing as one pleases; yet, the actual effect upon human behavior may threaten the survival of a culture. The enormous potential of those who have nothing to do cannot be overlooked. They may be productive or destructive, conserving or consuming. They may reach the limits of their capacities or be converted into machines. They may support the culture if they are strongly reinforced by it or defect if life is boring. They may or may not be prepared to act effectively when leisure comes to an end.

Leisure is one of the great challenges to those who are concerned with the survival of a culture because any attempt to control what a person does when he does not need to do anything is particularly likely to be attacked as unwarranted meddling. Life, liberty, and the pursuit of happiness are basic rights. But they are the rights of the individual and were listed as such at a time when the literatures of freedom and dignity were concerned with the aggrandizement of the individual. They have only a minor bearing on the survival of a culture.

The designer of a culture is not an interloper or meddler. He does not step in to disturb a natural process, he is part of a natural process. The geneticist who changes the characteristics of a species by selective breeding or by changing genes may seem to be meddling in biological evolution, but he does so because his species has evolved to the point at which it has been able to develop a science of genetics and a culture which induces its members to take the future of the species into account.

Those who have been induced by their culture to act to further its survival through design must accept the fact that they are altering the conditions under which men live and, hence, engaging in the control of human behavior. Good government is as much a matter of the control of human behavior as bad, good incentive conditions as much as exploitation, good teaching as much as punitive drill. Nothing is to be gained by using a softer word. If we are content merely to "influence" people, we shall not get far from the original meaning of that word—"an ethereal fluid thought to flow from the stars and to affect the actions of men."

Attacking controlling practices is, of course, a form of countercontrol. It may have immeasurable benefits if better controlling practices are thereby selected. But the literatures of freedom and dignity have made the mistake of supposing that they are suppressing control rather than correcting it. The reciprocal control through which a culture evolves is then disturbed. To refuse to exercise available control because in some sense all control is wrong is to withhold possibly important forms of countercontrol. We have seen some of the consequences. Punitive measures, which the literatures of freedom and dignity have otherwise helped to eliminate, are instead promoted. A preference for methods which make control inconspicuous or allow it to be disguised has condemned those who are in a position to exert constructive countercontrol to the use of weak measures.

This could be a lethal cultural mutation. Our culture has produced the science and technology it needs to save itself. It has the wealth needed for effective action. It has, to a considerable extent, a concern for its own future. But if it continues to take freedom or dignity, rather than its own survival, as its principal value, then it is possible that some other culture will make a greater contribution to the future. The defender of freedom and dignity may then, like Milton's Satan, continue to tell himself that he has "a mind not to be changed by place or time" and an all-sufficient personal identity ("What matter where, if I be still the same?"), but he will nevertheless find himself in hell with no other consolation than the illusion that "here at least we shall be free."

* * *

A culture is like the experimental space used in the study of behavior. It is a set of contingencies of reinforcement, a concept which has only recently begun to be understood. The technology of behavior which emerges is ethically neutral, but when applied to the design of a culture, the survival of the culture functions as a value. Those who have been induced to work for their culture need to foresee some of the problems to be solved, but many current features of a culture have an obvious bearing on its survival value. The designs to be found in the utopian literature appeal to certain simplifying principles. They have the merit of emphasizing survival value: Will the utopia work? The world at large is, of course, much more complex, but the processes are the same and practices work for the same reasons. Above all, there is the same advantage in stating objectives in behavioral terms. The use of science in designing a culture is commonly opposed. It is said that the science is inadequate, that its use may have disastrous consequences, that it will not produce a culture which members of other cultures will like, and in any case that men will somehow refuse to be controlled. The misuse of a technology of behavior is a serious matter, but we can guard against it best by looking not at putative controllers but at the contingencies under which they control. It is not the benevolence of a controller but the contingencies under which he controls benevolently which must be examined. All control is reciprocal, and an interchange between control and countercontrol is essential to the evolution of a culture. The interchange is disturbed by the literatures of freedom and dignity, which interpret countercontrol as the suppression rather than the correction of controlling practices. The effect could be lethal. In spite of remarkable advantages, our culture may prove to have a fatal flaw. Some other culture may then make a greater contribution to the future.

9
What Is Man?

AS A SCIENCE OF BEHAVIOR adopts the strategy of physics and biology, the autonomous agent to which behavior has traditionally been attributed is replaced by the environment—the environment in which the species evolved and in which the behavior of the individual is shaped and maintained. The vicissitudes of "environmentalism" show how difficult it has been to make this change. That a man's behavior owes something to antecedent events and that the environment is a more promising point of attack than man himself has long been recognized. As Crane Brinton observed, "a program to change things not just to convert people" was a significant part of the English, French, and Russian revolutions. It was Robert Owen, according to Trevelyan, who first "clearly grasped and taught that environment makes character and that environment is under human control" or, as Gilbert Seldes wrote, "that man is a creature of circumstance, that if you changed the environments of thirty little Hottentots and thirty little aristocratic English children, the aristocrats would become Hottentots, for all practical purposes, and the Hottentots little conservatives."

The evidence for a crude environmentalism is clear enough. People are extraordinarily different in different places, and possibly just because of the places. The nomad on horseback in Outer Mongolia and the astronaut in outer space are different people, but, as far as we know, if they had been exchanged at birth, they would have taken each other's place. (The expression "change places" shows how closely we identify a person's behavior with the environment in which it occurs.) But we need to know a great deal more before that fact becomes useful. What is it about the environment that produces a Hottentot? And what would need to be changed to produce an English conservative instead?

Both the enthusiasm of the environmentalist and his usually ignominious failure are illustrated by Owen's utopian experiment at New Harmony. A long history of environmental reform—in education, penology, industry, and family life, not to mention government and religion—has shown the same pattern. Environments are constructed on the model of environments in which good behavior has been observed, but the behavior fails to appear. Two hundred years of this kind of environmentalism has very little to show for itself, and for a simple reason. We must know how the environment works before we can change it to change behavior. A mere shift in emphasis from man to environment means very little.

Let us consider some examples in which the environment takes over the function and role of autonomous man. The first, often said to involve human nature, is *aggression*. Men often act in such a way that they harm others, and they often seem to be reinforced by signs of damage to others. The ethologists have emphasized contingencies of survival which would contribute these features to the genetic endowment of the species, but the contingencies of reinforcement in the lifetime of the individual are also significant, since anyone who acts aggressively to harm others is likely to be reinforced in other ways—for example, by taking possession of goods. The contingencies explain the behavior quite apart from any state or feeling of aggression or any initiating act by autonomous man.

Another example involving a so-called "trait of character" is *industry*. Some people are industrious in the sense that they work energetically for long periods of time, while others are lazy and idle in the sense that they do not. "Industry" and "laziness" are among thousands of so-called "traits." The behavior they refer to can be explained in other ways. Some of it may be attributed to genetic idiosyncrasies (and subject to change only through genetic measures), and the rest to environmental contingencies, which are much more important than is usually realized. Regardless of any normal genetic endowment, an organism will range between vigorous activity and complete quiescence depending upon the schedules on which it has been reinforced. The explanation shifts from a trait of character to an environmental history of reinforcement.

A third example, a "cognitive" activity, is *attention*. A person responds only to a small part of the stimuli impinging upon him. The traditional view is that he himself determines which stimuli are to be effective by "paying attention" to them. Some kind of inner gatekeeper is said to allow some stimuli to enter and to keep all others out. A sudden or strong stimulus may break through and "attract" attention, but the person himself seems otherwise to be in control. An analysis of the environmental circumstances reverses the relation. The kinds of stimuli which break through by "attracting attention" do so because they have been associated in the evolutionary history of the species or the personal history of the individual with important—e.g., dangerous—things. Less forceful stimuli attract attention only to the extent that they have figured in contingencies of reinforcement. We can arrange contingencies which ensure that an organism—even such a "simple" organism as a pigeon—will attend to one object and not to another, or to one property of an object, such as its color, and not to another, such as its shape. The inner gatekeeper is replaced by the contingencies to which the organism has been exposed and which select the stimuli to which it reacts.

In the traditional view a person perceives the world around him and acts upon it to make it known to him. In a sense he reaches out and grasps it. He "takes it in" and possesses it. He "knows" it in the Biblical sense in which a man knows a woman. It has even been argued that the world would not exist if no one perceived it. The action is exactly reversed in an environmental analysis. There would, of course, be no perception if there were no world to be perceived, but an existing world would not be perceived if there were no appropriate contingencies. We say that a baby perceives his mother's face and knows it. Our evidence is that the baby responds in one way to his mother's face and in other ways to other faces or other things. He makes this distinction not through some mental act of perception but because of prior contingencies. Some of these may be contingencies of survival. Physical features of a species are particularly stable parts of the environment in which a species evolves. (That is why courtship and sex and relations between parent and offspring are given such a prominent place by ethologists.) The face and facial expressions of the human mother have been associated with security, warmth, food, and other important things, during both the evolution of the species and the life of the child.

We learn to perceive in the sense that we learn to respond to things in particular ways because of the contingencies of which they are a part. We may perceive the sun, for example, simply because it is an extremely powerful stimulus, but it has been a permanent part of the environment of the species throughout its evolution and more specific behavior with respect to it could have been selected by contingencies of survival (as it has been in many other species). The sun also figures in many current contingencies of reinforcement: we move into or out of sunlight depending on the temperature; we wait for the sun to rise or set to take practical action; we talk about the sun and its effects; and we eventually study the sun with the instruments and methods of science. Our perception of the sun depends on what we do with respect to it. Whatever we do, and hence however we perceive it, the fact remains that it is the environment which acts upon the perceiving person, not the perceiving person who acts upon the environment.

The perceiving and knowing which arise from verbal contingencies are even more obviously products of the environment. We react to an object in many practical ways because of its color; thus, we pick and eat red apples of a particular variety but not green. It is clear that we can "tell the difference" between red and green, but something more is involved when we say that we *know* that one apple is red and the other green. It is tempting to say that knowing is a cognitive process altogether divorced from action, but the contingencies provide a more useful distinction. When someone asks about the color of an object which he cannot see, and we tell him that it is red, *we* do nothing about the object in any other way. It is the person who has questioned us and heard our answer who makes a practical response which depends on color. Only under verbal contingencies can a speaker respond to an isolated property to which a nonverbal response cannot be made. A response made to the property of an object without responding to the object in any other way is called *abstract*. Abstract thinking is the product of a particular kind of environment, not of a cognitive faculty.

As listeners we acquire a kind of knowledge from the verbal behavior of others which may be extremely valuable in permitting us to avoid direct exposure to contingencies. We learn from the experience of others by responding to what they say about contingencies. When we are warned against doing something or are advised to do something, there may be no point in speaking of knowledge, but when we learn more durable kinds of warnings and advice in the form of maxims or rules, we may be said to have a special kind of knowledge about the contingencies to which they apply. The laws of science are descriptions of contingencies of reinforcement, and one who knows a scientific law may behave effectively without being exposed to the contingencies it describes. (He will, of course, have very different feelings about the contingencies, depending on whether he is following a rule or has been directly exposed to them. Scientific knowledge is "cold," but the behavior to which it gives rise is as effective as the "warm" knowledge which comes from personal experience.)

Isaiah Berlin has referred to a particular sense of knowing, said to have been discovered by Giambattista Vico. It is "the sense in which I know what it is to be poor, to fight for a cause, belong to a nation, to join or abandon a church or a party, to feel nostalgia, terror, the omnipresence of a god, to understand a gesture, a work of art, a joke, a man's character, that one is transformed or lying to oneself." These are the kinds of things one is likely to learn through direct contact with contingencies rather than from the verbal behavior of others, and special kinds of feelings are no doubt associated with them, but, even so, the knowledge is not somehow directly given. A person can know what it is to fight for a cause only after a long history during which he has learned to perceive and to know that state of affairs called fighting for a cause.

The role of the environment is particularly subtle when what is known is the knower himself. If there is no external world to initiate knowing, must we not then say that the knower himself acts first? This is, of course, the field of consciousness, or awareness, a field which a scientific analysis of behavior is often accused of ignoring. The charge is a serious one and should be taken seriously. Man is said to differ from the other animals mainly because he is "aware of his own existence." He knows what he is doing; he knows that he has had a past and will have a future; he "reflects on his own nature"; he alone follows the classical injunction "Know thyself." Any analysis of human behavior which neglected these facts would be defective indeed. And some analyses do. What is called "methodological behaviorism" limits itself to what can be publicly observed; mental processes may exist, but they are ruled out of scientific consideration by their nature. The "behavioralists" in political science and many logical positivists in philosophy have followed a similar line. But self-observation can be studied, and it must be included in any reasonably complete account of human behavior. Rather than ignore consciousness, an experimental analysis of behavior has stressed certain crucial issues. The question is not whether a man can know himself but what he knows when he does so.

The problem arises in part from the indisputable fact of privacy: a small part of the universe is enclosed

within a human skin. It would be foolish to deny the
existence of that private world, but it is also foolish to
assert that because it is private it is of a different
nature from the world outside. The difference is not
in the stuff of which the private world is composed,
but in its accessibility. There is an exclusive intimacy
about a headache, or heartache, or a silent soliloquy.
The intimacy is sometimes distressing (one cannot shut
one's eyes to a headache), but it need not be, and it
has seemed to support the doctrine that knowing is a
kind of possession.

The difficulty is that although privacy may bring the
knower closer to what he knows, it interferes with the
process through which he comes to know anything. As
we saw in Chapter 6, the contingencies under which a
child learns to describe his feelings are necessarily
defective; the verbal community cannot use the procedures with which it teaches a child to describe objects.
There are, of course, natural contingencies under which
we learn to respond to private stimuli, and they generate behavior of great precision; we could not jump
or walk or turn a handspring if we were not being
stimulated by parts of our own body. But very little
awareness is associated with this kind of behavior and,
in fact, we behave in these ways most of the time without being aware of the stimuli to which we are responding. We do not attribute awareness to other species
which obviously use similar private stimuli. To "know"
private stimuli is more than to respond to them.

The verbal community specializes in self-descriptive
contingencies. It asks such questions as: What did you
do yesterday? What are you doing now? What will you
do tomorrow? Why did you do that? Do you really
want to do that? How do you feel about that? The
answers help people to adjust to each other effectively.
And it is because such questions are asked that a per-

son responds to himself and his behavior in the special way called knowing or being aware. Without the help of a verbal community all behavior would be unconscious. Consciousness is a social product. It is not only *not* the special field of autonomous man, it is not within range of a solitary man.

And it is not within the range of accuracy of anyone. The privacy which seems to confer intimacy upon self-knowledge makes it impossible for the verbal community to maintain precise contingencies. Introspective vocabularies are by nature inaccurate, and that is one reason why they have varied so widely among schools of philosophy and psychology. Even a carefully trained observer runs into trouble when new private stimuli are studied. (Independent evidence of private stimulation—for example, through physiological measures—would make it possible to sharpen the contingencies which generate self-observation and would, incidentally, confirm the present interpretation. Such evidence would not, as we noted in Chapter 1, offer any support for a theory which attributed human behavior to an observable inner agent.)

Theories of psychotherapy which emphasize awareness assign a role to autonomous man which is properly, and much more effectively, reserved for contingencies of reinforcement. Awareness may help if the problem is in part a lack of awareness, and "insight" into one's condition may help if one then takes remedial action, but awareness or insight alone is not always enough, and it may be too much. One need not be aware of one's behavior or the conditions controlling it in order to behave effectively—or ineffectively. On the contrary, as the toad's inquiry of the centipede demonstrates, constant self-observation may be a handicap. The accomplished pianist would perform badly if he were as clearly aware of his behavior as the student who is just learning to play.

Cultures are often judged by the extent to which they encourage self-observation. Some cultures are said to breed unthinking men, and Socrates has been admired for inducing men to inquire into their own nature, but self-observation is only a preliminary to action. The extent to which a man *should* be aware of himself depends upon the importance of self-observation for effective behavior. Self-knowledge is valuable only to the extent that it helps to meet the contingencies under which it has arisen.

Perhaps the last stronghold of autonomous man is that complex "cognitive" activity called thinking. Because it is complex, it has yielded only slowly to explanation in terms of contingencies of reinforcement. When we say that a person *discriminates* between red and orange, we imply that discrimination is a kind of mental act. The person himself does not seem to be doing anything; he responds in different ways to red and orange stimuli, but this is the result of discrimination rather than the act. Similarly, we say that a person *generalizes* —say, from his own limited experience to the world at large—but all we see is that he responds to the world at large as he has learned to respond to his own small world. We say that a person *forms a concept or an abstraction,* but all we see is that certain kinds of contingencies of reinforcement have brought a response under the control of a single property of a stimulus. We say that a person *recalls* or *remembers* what he has seen or heard, but all we see is that the present occasion evokes a response, possibly in weakened or altered form, acquired on another occasion. We say that a person *associates* one word with another, but all we observe is that one verbal stimulus evokes the response

previously made to another. Rather than suppose that
it is therefore autonomous man who discriminates,
generalizes, forms concepts or abstractions, recalls or
remembers, and associates, we can put matters in good
order simply by noting that these terms do not refer
to forms of behavior.

A person may take explicit action, however, when he
solves a problem. In putting a jigsaw puzzle together he
may move the pieces around to improve his chances of
finding a fit. In solving an equation he may transpose,
clear fractions, and extract roots to improve his chances
of finding a form of the equation he has already learned
how to solve. The creative artist may manipulate a
medium until something of interest turns up. Much of
this can be done covertly, and it is then likely to be
assigned to a different dimensional system, but it can
always be done overtly, perhaps more slowly but
also often more effectively, and with rare exceptions
it must have been learned in overt form. The culture
promotes thinking by constructing special contingencies. It teaches a person to make fine discriminations
by making differential reinforcement more precise. It
teaches techniques to be used in solving problems.
It provides rules which make it unnecessary to be
exposed to the contingences from which the rules are
derived, and it provides rules for finding rules.

Self-control, or self-management, is a special kind of
problem solving which, like self-knowledge, raises all
the issues associated with privacy. We have discussed
some techniques in connection with aversive control in
Chapter 4. It is always the environment which builds
the behavior with which problems are solved, even
when the problems are to be found in the private world
inside the skin. None of this has been investigated in a
very productive way, but the inadequacy of our analysis is no reason to fall back on a miracle-working

mind. If our understanding of contingencies of reinforcement is not yet sufficient to explain all kinds of
thinking, we must remember that the appeal to mind
explains nothing at all.

In shifting control from autonomous man to the
observable environment we do not leave an empty
organism. A great deal goes on inside the skin, and
physiology will eventually tell us more about it. It will
explain why behavior is indeed related to the antecedent events of which it can be shown to be a function.
The assignment is not always correctly understood.
Many physiologists regard themselves as looking for
the "physiological correlates" of mental events. Physiological research is regarded as simply a more scientific
version of introspection. But physiological techniques
are not, of course, designed to detect or measure personalities, ideas, attitudes, feelings, impulses, thoughts,
or purposes. (If they were, we should have to answer
a third question in addition to those raised in Chapter 1: How can a personality, idea, feeling, or purpose
affect the instruments of the physiologist?) At the
moment neither introspection nor physiology supplies
very adequate information about what is going on inside a man as he behaves, and since they are both
directed inward, they have the same effect of diverting
attention from the external environment.

Much of the misunderstanding about an inner man
comes from the metaphor of storage. Evolutionary and
environmental histories change an organism, but they
are not stored within it. Thus, we observe that babies
suck their mothers' breasts, and we can easily imagine
that a strong tendency to do so has survival value, but
much more is implied by a "sucking instinct" regarded
as something a baby possesses which enables it to suck.
The concept of "human nature" or "genetic endowment" is dangerous when taken in that sense. We are

closer to human nature in a baby than in an adult, or in a primitive culture than in an advanced, in the sense that environmental contingencies are less likely to have obscured the genetic endowment, and it is tempting to dramatize that endowment by implying that earlier stages have survived in concealed form: man is a naked ape, and "the paleolithic bull which survives in man's inner self still paws the earth whenever a threatening gesture is made on the social scene." But anatomists and physiologists will not find an ape, or a bull, or for that matter instincts. They will find anatomical and physiological features which are the product of an evolutionary history.

The personal history of the individual is also often said to be stored within him. For "instinct" read "habit." The cigarette habit is presumably something more than the behavior said to show that a person possesses it; but the only other information we have concerns the reinforcers and the schedules of reinforcement which make a person smoke a great deal. The contingencies are not stored; they have simply left a changed person.

The environment is often said to be stored in the form of memories: to recall something we search for a copy of it, which can then be seen as the original thing was seen. As far as we know, however, there are no copies of the environment in the individual *at any time*, even when a thing is present and being observed. The products of more complex contingencies are also said to be stored; the repertoire acquired as a person learns to speak French is called a "knowledge of French."

Traits of character, whether derived from contingencies of survival or contingencies of reinforcement, are also said to be stored. A curious example occurs in Follett's *Modern American Usage:* "We say *He faced*

these adversities bravely, aware without thought that
the bravery is a property of the man, not of the facing;
a brave act is poetic shorthand for the act of a person
who shows bravery by performing it." But we call a
man brave because of his acts, and he behaves bravely
when environmental circumstances induce him to do
so. The circumstances have changed his behavior; they
have not implanted a trait or virtue.

Philosophies are also spoken of as things possessed.
A man is said to speak or act in certain ways because
he has a particular philosophy—such as idealism, dia-
lectical materialism, or Calvinism. Terms of this kind
summarize the effect of environmental conditions which
it would now be hard to trace, but the conditions must
have existed and should not be ignored. A person who
possesses a "philosophy of freedom" is one who has
been changed in certain ways by the literature of
freedom.

The issue has had a curious place in theology. Does
man sin because he is sinful, or is he sinful because he
sins? Neither question points to anything very useful.
To say that a man is sinful because he sins is to give
an operational definition of sin. To say that he sins
because he is sinful is to trace his behavior to a supposed inner trait. But whether or not a person engages
in the kind of behavior called sinful depends upon
circumstances which are not mentioned in either question. The sin assigned as an inner possession (the sin
a person "knows") is to be found in a history of reinforcement. (The expression "God-fearing" suggests
such a history, but piety, virtue, the immanence of
God, a moral sense, or morality does not. As we have
seen, man is not a moral animal in the sense of possessing a special trait or virtue; he has built a kind of social
environment which induces him to behave in moral
ways.)

These distinctions have practical implications. A recent survey of white Americans is said to have shown that "more than half blamed the inferior educational and economic status of blacks on 'something about Negroes themselves.'" The "something" was further identified as "lack of motivation," which was to be distinguished from *both* genetic and environmental factors. Significantly, motivation was said to be associated with "free will." To neglect the role of the environment in this way is to discourage any inquiry into the defective contingencies responsible for a "lack of motivation."

It is in the nature of an experimental analysis of human behavior that it should strip away the functions previously assigned to autonomous man and transfer them one by one to the controlling environment. The analysis leaves less and less for autonomous man to do. But what about man himself? Is there not something about a person which is more than a living body? Unless something called a self survives, how can we speak of self-knowledge or self-control? To whom is the injunction "Know thyself" addressed?

It is an important part of the contingencies to which a young child is exposed that his own body is the only part of his environment which remains the same (*idem*) from moment to moment and day to day. We say that he discovers his *identity* as he learns to distinguish between his body and the rest of the world. He does this long before the community teaches him to call things by name and to distinguish "me" from "it" or "you."

A self is a repertoire of behavior appropriate to a given set of contingencies. A substantial part of the conditions to which a person is exposed may play a dominant role, and under other conditions a person may report, "I'm not myself today," or, "I couldn't have done what you said I did, because that's not like me." The identity conferred upon a self arises from the contingencies responsible for the behavior. Two or more repertoires generated by different sets of contingencies compose two or more selves. A person possesses one repertoire appropriate to his life with his friends and another appropriate to his life with his family, and a friend may find him a very different person if he sees him with his family or his family if they see him with his friends. The problem of identity arises when situations are intermingled, as when a person finds himself with both his family and his friends at the same time.

Self-knowledge and self-control imply two selves in this sense. The self-knower is almost always a product of social contingencies, but the self that is known may come from other sources. The controlling self (the conscience or superego) is of social origin, but the controlled self is more likely to be the product of genetic susceptibilities to reinforcement (the id, or the Old Adam). The controlling self generally represents the interests of others, the controlled self the interests of the individual.

The picture which emerges from a scientific analysis is not of a body with a person inside, but of a body which *is* a person in the sense that it displays a complex repertoire of behavior. The picture is, of course, unfamiliar. The man thus portrayed is a stranger, and from the traditional point of view he may not seem to be a man at all. "For at least one hundred years," said Joseph Wood Krutch, "we have been prejudiced in every theory, including economic determinism, mechanistic behaviorism, and relativism, that reduces the stature of man until he ceases to be man at all in any sense that the humanists of an earlier generation would recognize." Matson has argued that "the empirical behavioral scientist . . . denies, if only by implication, that a unique being, called Man, exists." "What is now under attack," said Maslow, "is the 'being' of man." C. S. Lewis put it quite bluntly: Man is being abolished.

There is clearly some difficulty in identifying the man to whom these expressions refer. Lewis cannot have meant the human species, for not only is it not being abolished, it is filling the earth. (As a result it may eventually abolish itself through disease, famine, pollution, or a nuclear holocaust, but that is not what Lewis meant.) Nor are individual men growing less effective or productive. We are told that what is threatened is "man *qua* man," or "man in his humanity," or "man as Thou not It," or "man as a person not a thing." These are not very helpful expressions, but they supply a clue. What is being abolished is autonomous man— the inner man, the homunculus, the possessing demon, the man defended by the literatures of freedom and dignity.

His abolition has long been overdue. Autonomous man is a device used to explain what we cannot explain in any other way. He has been constructed from our ignorance, and as our understanding increases, the very stuff of which he is composed vanishes. Science does not dehumanize man, it de-homunculizes him, and it must do so if it is to prevent the abolition of the human species. To man *qua* man we readily say good riddance. Only by dispossessing him can we turn to the real causes of human behavior. Only then can we turn from the inferred to the observed, from the miraculous to the natural, from the inaccessible to the manipulable.

It is often said that in doing so we must treat the man who survives as a mere animal. "Animal" is a pejorative term, but only because "man" has been made

spuriously honorific. Krutch has argued that whereas
the traditional view supports Hamlet's exclamation,
"How like a god!," Pavlov, the behavioral scientist,
emphasized "How like a dog!" But that was a step
forward. A god is the archetypal pattern of an explanatory fiction, of a miracle-working mind, of the meta-
physical. Man is much more than a dog, but like a dog
he is within range of a scientific analysis.

It is true that much of the experimental analysis of
behavior has been concerned with lower organisms.
Genetic differences are minimized by using special
strains; environmental histories can be controlled, perhaps from birth; strict regimens can be maintained
during long experiments; and very little of this is
possible with human subjects. Moreover, in working
with lower animals the scientist is less likely to put his
own responses to the experimental conditions among
his data, or to design contingencies with an eye to their
effect on him rather than on the experimental organism he is studying. No one is disturbed when physiologists study respiration, reproduction, nutrition, or
endocrine systems in animals; they do so to take advantage of very great similarities. Comparable similarities
in behavior are being discovered. There is, of course,
always the danger that methods designed for the study
of lower animals will emphasize only those characteristics which they have in common with men, but we
cannot discover what is "essentially" human until we
have investigated nonhuman subjects. Traditional theories of autonomous man have exaggerated species
differences. Some of the complex contingencies of reinforcement now under investigation generate behavior
in lower organisms which, if the subjects were human,
would traditionally be said to involve higher mental
processes.

Man is not made into a machine by analyzing his

behavior in mechanical terms. Early theories of behavior, as we have seen, represented man as a push-pull automaton, close to the nineteenth-century notion of a machine, but progress has been made. Man is a machine in the sense that he is a complex system behaving in lawful ways, but the complexity is extraordinary. His capacity to adjust to contingencies of reinforcement will perhaps be eventually simulated by machines, but this has not yet been done, and the living system thus simulated will remain unique in other ways.

Nor is man made into a machine by inducing him to use machines. Some machines call for behavior which is repetitious and monotonous, and we escape from them when we can, but others enormously extend our effectiveness in dealing with the world around us. A person may respond to very small things with the help of an electron microscope and to very large things with radiotelescopes, and in doing so he may seem quite inhuman to those who use only their unaided senses. A person may act upon the environment with the delicate precision of a micromanipulator or with the range and power of a space rocket, and his behavior may seem inhuman to those who rely only on muscular contractions. (It has been argued that the apparatus used in the operant laboratory misrepresents natural behavior because it introduces an external source of power, but men use external sources when they fly kites, sail boats, or shoot bows and arrows. They would have to abandon all but a small fraction of their achievements if they used only the power of their muscles.) People record their behavior in books and other media, and the use they make of the records may seem quite inhuman to those who can use only what they remember. People describe complex contingencies in the form of rules, and rules for manipulating rules, and they introduce them into electronic systems which "think" with a speed that seems quite inhuman to the unaided thinker. Human beings do all this with machines, and they would be less than human if they did not. What we now regard as machine-like behavior was, in fact, much commoner before the invention of these devices. The slave in the cotton field, the book-keeper on his high stool, the student being drilled by a teacher—these were the machine-like men.

Machines replace people when they do what people have done, and the social consequences may be serious. As technology advances, machines will take over more and more of the functions of men, but only up to a point. We build machines which reduce some of the aversive features of our environment (grueling labor, for example) and which produce more positive rein-forcers. We build them precisely because they do so. We have no reason to build machines to be reinforced by these consequences, and to do so would be to deprive ourselves of reinforcement. If the machines man makes eventually make him wholly expendable, it will be by accident, not design.

An important role of autonomous man has been to give human behavior direction, and it is often said that in dispossessing an inner agent we leave man himself without a purpose. As one writer has put it, "Since a scientific psychology must regard human behavior objectively, as determined by necessary laws, it must represent human behavior as unintentional." But "neces-sary laws" would have this effect only if they referred exclusively to antecedent conditions. Intention and purpose refer to selective consequences, the effects of which can be formulated in "necessary laws." Has life, in all the forms in which it exists on the surface of the earth, a purpose, and is this evidence of intentional design? The primate hand evolved *in order that* things might be more successfully manipulated, but its purpose is to be found not in a prior design but rather in the process of selection. Similarly, in operant conditioning the purpose of a skilled movement of the hand is to be found in the consequences which follow it. A pianist neither acquires nor executes the behavior of playing a scale smoothly because of a prior intention of doing so. Smoothly played scales are reinforcing for many reasons, and they select skilled movements. In neither the evolution of the human hand nor in the acquired use of the hand is any prior intention or purpose at issue.

The argument for purpose seems to be strengthened by moving back into the darker recesses of mutation. Jacques Barzun has argued that Darwin and Marx both neglected not only human purpose but the creative purpose responsible for the variations upon which natural selection plays. It may prove to be the case, as some geneticists have argued, that mutations are not entirely random, but nonrandomness is not necessarily the proof of a creative mind. Mutations will not be random when geneticists explicitly design them in order that an organism will meet specific conditions of selection more successfully, and geneticists will then seem to be playing the role of the creative Mind in pre-evolutionary theory, but the purpose they display will have to be sought in their culture, in the social environment which has induced them to make genetic changes appropriate to contingencies of survival.

There is a difference between biological and individual purpose in that the latter can be felt. No one could have felt the purpose in the development of the human hand, whereas a person can in a sense feel the purpose with which he plays a smooth scale. But he does not play a smooth scale *because* he feels the pur-

pose of doing so; what he feels is a by-product of his
behavior in relation to its consequences. The relation
of the human hand to the contingencies of survival
under which it evolved is, of course, out of reach of
personal observation; the relation of the behavior to
contingencies of reinforcement which have generated
it is not.

A scientific analysis of behavior dispossesses autonomous man and turns the control he has been said to
exert over to the environment. The individual may
then seem particularly vulnerable. He is henceforth to
be controlled by the world around him, and in large
part by other men. Is he not then simply a victim?
Certainly men have been victims, as they have been
victimizers, but the word is too strong. It implies
despoliation, which is by no means an essential consequence of interpersonal control. But even under
benevolent control is the individual not at best a spectator who may watch what happens but is helpless to
do anything about it? Is he not "at a dead end in his
long struggle to control his own destiny"?

It is only autonomous man who has reached a dead
end. Man himself may be controlled by his environment, but it is an environment which is almost wholly
of his own making. The physical environment of most
people is largely man-made. The surfaces a person
walks on, the walls which shelter him, the clothing he
wears, many of the foods he eats, the tools he uses, the
vehicles he moves about in, most of the things he
listens to and looks at are human products. The social
environment is obviously man-made—it generates the
language a person speaks, the customs he follows, and
the behavior he exhibits with respect to the ethical,
religious, governmental, economic, educational, and
psychotherapeutic institutions which control him. The

evolution of a culture is in fact a kind of gigantic exercise in self-control. As the individual controls himself by manipulating the world in which he lives, so the human species has constructed an environment in which its members behave in a highly effective way. Mistakes have been made, and we have no assurance that the environment man has constructed will continue to provide gains which outstrip the losses, but man as we know him, for better or for worse, is what man has made of man.

This will not satisfy those who cry "Victim!" C. S. Lewis protested: ". . . the power of man to make himself what he pleases . . . means . . . the power of some men to make other men what they please." This is inevitable in the nature of cultural evolution. The controlling *self* must be distinguished from the controlled self, even when they are both inside the same skin, and when control is exercised through the design of an external environment, the selves are, with minor exceptions, distinct. The person who unintentionally or intentionally introduces a new cultural practice is only one among possibly billions who will be affected by it. If this does not seem like an act of self-control, it is only because we have misunderstood the nature of self-control in the individual.

When a person changes his physical or social environment "intentionally"—that is, in order to change human behavior, possibly including his own—he plays two roles: one as a controller, as the designer of a controlling culture, and another as the controlled, as the product of a culture. There is nothing inconsistent about this; it follows from the nature of the evolution of a culture, with or without intentional design.

The human species has probably not undergone much genetic change in recorded time. We have only to go back a thousand generations to reach the artists of the caves of Lascaux. Features which bear directly on survival (such as resistance to disease) change substantially in a thousand generations, but the child of one of the Lascaux artists transplanted to the world of today might be almost indistinguishable from a modern child. It is possible that he would learn more slowly than his modern counterpart, that he could maintain only a smaller repertoire without confusion, or that he would forget more quickly; we cannot be sure. But we can be sure that a twentieth-century child transplanted to the civilization of Lascaux would not be very different from the children he met there, for we have seen what happens when a modern child is raised in an impoverished environment.

Man has greatly changed himself as a person in the same period of time by changing the world in which he lives. Something of the order of a hundred generations will cover the development of modern religious practices, and something of the same order of magnitude modern government and law. Perhaps no more than twenty generations will account for modern industrial practices, and possibly no more than four or five for education and psychotherapy. The physical and biological technologies which have increased man's sensitivity to the world around him and his power to change that world have taken no more than four or five generations.

Man has "controlled his own destiny," if that expression means anything at all. The man that man has made is the product of the culture man has devised. He has emerged from two quite different processes of evolution: the biological evolution responsible for the human species and the cultural evolution carried out by that species. Both of these processes of evolution may now accelerate because they are both subject to intentional design. Men have already changed their genetic endowment by breeding selectively and by changing contingencies of survival, and they may now begin to introduce mutations directly related to survival. For a long time men have introduced new practices which serve as cultural mutations, and they have changed the conditions under which practices are selected. They may now begin to do both with a clearer eye to the consequences.

Man will presumably continue to change, but we cannot say in what direction. No one could have predicted the evolution of the human species at any point in its early history, and the direction of intentional genetic design will depend upon the evolution of a culture which is itself unpredictable for similar reasons. "The limits of perfection of the human species," said Étienne Cabet in *Voyage en Icarie*, "are as yet unknown." But, of course, there are no limits. The human species will never reach a final state of perfection before it is exterminated—"some say in fire, some in ice," and some in radiation.

The individual occupies a place in a culture not unlike his place in the species, and in early evolutionary theory that place was hotly debated. Was the species simply a type of individual, and if so, in what sense could it evolve? Darwin himself declared species "to be purely subjective inventions of the taxonomist." A species has no existence except as a collection of individuals, nor has a family, tribe, race, nation, or class. A culture has no existence apart from the behavior of the individuals who maintain its practices. It is always an individual who behaves, who acts upon the environment and is changed by the consequences of his action, and who maintains the social contingencies which *are* a culture. The individual is the carrier of both his species and his culture. Cultural practices, like genetic traits, are transmitted from individual to individual. A new practice, like a new genetic trait, appears first in an individual and tends to be transmitted if it contributes to his survival as an individual.

Yet, the individual is at best a locus in which many lines of development come together in a unique set. His individuality is unquestioned. Every cell in his body is a unique genetic product, as unique as that classic mark of individuality, the fingerprint. And even within the most regimented culture every personal history is unique. No intentional culture can destroy that uniqueness, and, as we have seen, any effort to do so would be bad design. But the individual nevertheless remains merely a stage in a process which began long before he came into existence and will long outlast him. He has no ultimate responsibility for a species trait or a cultural practice, even though it was he who underwent the mutation or introduced the practice which became part of the species or culture. Even if Lamarck had been right in supposing that the individual could change his genetic structure through personal effort, we should have to point to the environmental circumstances responsible for the effort, as we shall have to do when geneticists begin to change the human endowment. And when an individual engages in the intentional design of a cultural practice, we must turn to the culture which induces him to do so and supplies the art or science he uses.

One of the great problems of individualism, seldom recognized as such, is death—the inescapable fate of the individual, the final assault on freedom and dignity. Death is one of those remote events which are brought to bear on behavior only with the aid of cultural practices. What we see is the death of others, as in Pascal's famous metophor: "Imagine a number of men in chains, all under sentence of death, some of whom are each day butchered in the sight of the others; those remaining see their own condition in that of their fellows, and looking at each other with grief and despair await their turn. This is an image of the human condition." Some religions have made death more important by picturing a future existence in heaven or hell, but the individualist has a special reason to fear death, engineered not by a religion but by the literatures of freedom and dignity. It is the prospect of personal annihilation. The individualist can find no solace in reflecting upon any contribution which will survive him. He has refused to act for the good of others and is therefore not reinforced by the fact that others whom he has helped will outlive him. He has refused to be concerned for the survival of his culture and is not reinforced by the fact that the culture will long survive him. In the defense of his own freedom and dignity he has denied the contributions of the past and must therefore relinquish all claim upon the future.

Science has probably never demanded a more sweeping change in a traditional way of thinking about a subject, nor has there ever been a more important subject. In the traditional picture a person perceives the world around him, selects features to be perceived, discriminates among them, judges them good or bad, changes them to make them better (or, if he is careless, worse), and may be held responsible for his action and justly rewarded or punished for its consequences. In the scientific picture a person is a member of a species shaped by evolutionary contingencies of survival, displaying behavioral processes which bring him under the control of the environment in which he lives, and largely under the control of a social environment which he and millions of others like him have constructed and maintained during the evolution of a culture. The direction of the controlling relation is reversed: a person does not act upon the world, the world acts upon him.

It is difficult to accept such a change simply on intellectual grounds and nearly impossible to accept its implications. The reaction of the traditionalist is usually described in terms of feelings. One of these, to which the Freudians have appealed in explaining the resistance to psychoanalysis, is wounded vanity. Freud himself expounded, as Ernest Jones has said, "the three heavy blows which narcissism or self-love of mankind had suffered at the hands of science. The first was cosmological and was dealt by Copernicus; the second was biological and was dealt by Darwin; the third was psychological and was dealt by Freud." (The blow was suffered by the belief that something at the center of man knows all that goes on within him and that an instrument called will power exercises command and control over the rest of one's personality.) But what are the signs or symptoms of wounded vanity, and how shall we explain them? What people *do* about such a scientific picture of man is call it wrong, demeaning, and dangerous, argue against it, and attack those who propose or defend it. They do so not out of wounded vanity but because the scientific formulation has destroyed accustomed reinforcers. If a person can no longer take credit or be admired for what he does, then he seems to suffer a loss of dignity or worth, and behavior previously reinforced by credit or admiration will undergo extinction. Extinction often leads to aggressive attack.

Another effect of the scientific picture has been described as a loss of faith or "nerve," as a sense of doubt or powerlessness, or as discouragement, depression, or despondency. A person is said to feel that he can do nothing about his own destiny. But what he feels is a weakening of old responses which are no longer reinforced. People are indeed "powerless" when long-established verbal repertoires prove useless. For example, one historian has complained that if the deeds of men are "to be dismissed as simply the product of material and psychological conditioning," there is nothing to write about; "change must be at least partially the result of conscious mental activity."

Another effect is a kind of nostalgia. Old repertoires break through, as similarities between present and past are seized upon and exaggerated. Old days are called the good old days, when the inherent dignity of man and the importance of spiritual values were recognized. Such fragments of outmoded behavior tend to be "wistful"—that is, they have the character of increasingly unsuccessful behavior.

These reactions to a scientific conception of man are certainly unfortunate. They immobilize men of good will, and anyone concerned with the future of his culture will do what he can to correct them. No theory changes what it is a theory about. Nothing is changed because we look at it, talk about it, or analyze it in a new way. Keats drank confusion to Newton for analyzing the rainbow, but the rainbow remained as beautiful as ever and became for many even more beautiful. Man has not changed because we look at him, talk about him, and analyze him scientifically. His achievements in science, government, religion, art, and literature remain as they have always been, to be admired as one admires a storm at sea or autumn foliage or a mountain peak, quite apart from their origins and untouched by a scientific analysis. What does change is our chance of doing something about the subject of a theory. Newton's analysis of the light in a rainbow was a step in the direction of the laser.

The traditional conception of man is flattering; it confers reinforcing privileges. It is therefore easily defended and can be changed only with difficulty. It was designed to build up the individual as an instrument of countercontrol, and it did so effectively but in such a way as to limit progress. We have seen how the literatures of freedom and dignity, with their concern for autonomous man, have perpetuated the use of punishment and condoned the use of only weak nonpunitive techniques, and it is not difficult to demonstrate a connection between the unlimited right of the individual to pursue happiness and the catastrophes threatened by unchecked breeding, the unrestrained affluence which exhausts resources and pollutes the environment, and the imminence of nuclear war.

Physical and biological technologies have alleviated pestilence and famine and many painful, dangerous, and exhausting features of daily life, and behavioral technology can begin to alleviate other kinds of ills. In the analysis of human behavior it is just possible that we are slightly beyond Newton's position in the analysis of light, for we are beginning to make technological applications. There are wonderful possibilities—and all the more wonderful because traditional approaches have been so ineffective. It is hard to imagine a world in which people live together without quarreling, maintain themselves by producing the food, shelter, and clothing they need, enjoy themselves and contribute to the enjoyment of others in art, music, literature, and games, consume only a reasonable part of the resources of the world and add as little as possible to its pollution, bear no more children than can be raised decently, continue to explore the world around them and discover better ways of dealing with it, and come to know themselves accurately and, therefore, manage themselves effectively. Yet all this is possible, and even the slightest sign of progress should bring a kind of change which in traditional terms would be said to assuage wounded vanity, offset a sense of hopelessness or nostalgia, correct the impression that "we neither can nor need to do anything for ourselves," and promote a "sense of freedom and dignity" by building "a sense of confidence and worth." In other words, it should abundantly reinforce those who have been induced by their culture to work for its survival.

* * *

An experimental analysis shifts the determination of behavior from autonomous man to the environment—an environment responsible both for the evolution of the species and for the repertoire acquired by each member. Early versions of environmentalism were inadequate because they could not explain how the environment worked, and much seemed to be left for autonomous man to do. But environmental contingencies now take over functions once attributed to autonomous man, and certain questions arise. Is man then "abolished"? Certainly not as a species or as an individual achiever. It is the autonomous inner man who is abolished, and that is a step forward. But does man not then become merely a victim or passive observer of what is happening to him? He is indeed controlled by his environment, but we must remember that it is an environment largely of his own making. The evolution of a culture is a gigantic exercise in self-control. It is often said that a scientific view of man leads to wounded vanity, a sense of hopelessness, and nostalgia. But no theory changes what it is a theory about; man remains what he has always been. And a new theory may change what can be done with its subject matter. A scientific view of man offers exciting possibilities. We have not yet seen what man can make of man.

Notes

REFERENCES CITED in the text and additional comments appear below, together with references to further discussions of certain topics in other books by the writer, identified as follows:

BO   *The Behavior of Organisms: An Experimental Analysis* (New York: Appleton-Century-Crofts, 1938)

WT   *Walden Two* (New York: Macmillan, 1948)

SHB   *Science and Human Behavior* (New York: Macmillan, 1953)

VB   *Verbal Behavior* (New York: Appleton-Century-Crofts, 1957)

SR   *Schedules of Reinforcement*, with Charles B. Ferster (New York: Appleton-Century-Crofts, 1957)

CR   *Cumulative Record, Revised Edition* (New York: Appleton-Century-Crofts, 1961)

TT   *The Technology of Teaching* (New York: Appleton-Century-Crofts, 1968)

COR   *Contingencies of Reinforcement: A Theoretical Analysis* (New York: Appleton-Century-Crofts, 1969)

The code at the left of entries indicates page number and line number of the materials described.

1 / 22   C. D. Darlington, *The Evolution of Man and Society.* Quoted in *Science*, 1970, *168*, 1332.

5 / 16   "cause". What is no longer common in sophisticated scientific writing is the push-pull causality of nineteenth-century science. The causes referred to here are, technically speaking, the independent variables of which behavior as a dependent variable is a function. See *SHB*, chap. 3.

5 / 24   On "possession," see *COR*, chap. 9.

6 / 12   Herbert Butterfield, *The Origins of Modern Science* (London: 1957).

8 / 18   Karl R. Popper, *Of Clouds and Clocks* (St. Louis: Washington University Press, 1966), p. 15.

8 / 25   Eric Robertson Dodds, *The Greeks and the Irrational* (Berkeley: University of California Press, 1951).

9 / 35   mind and behavior   See *COR*, chap. 8.

10 / 33 William James, "What Is an Emotion?" *Mind*, 1884, 9, 188–205.

14 / 23 the role of the environment   See *COR*, chap. 1.

14 / 28 René Descartes, *Traité de l'homme* (1662).

15 / 26 "prodded and lashed through life"   E. B. Holt, *Animal Drive and the Learning Process* (New York: Henry Holt & Co., 1931).

16 / 14 "operant" behavior   See *SHB*, chap. 5.

16 / 28 practical applications of operant behavior   See Roger Ulrich, Thomas Stachnik, and John Mabry, eds., *Control of Human Behavior*, vols. 1 and 2 (Glenview, Ill.: Scott, Foresman & Co., 1966 and 1970).

18 / 28 Joseph Wood Krutch, *New York Times Magazine*, July 30, 1967.

24 / 26 operant conditioning   See *SHB*, chaps. 5 and 11.

27 / 17 On shock-induced aggression, see N. H. Azrin, R. R. Hutchinson, and R. D. Sallery, "Pain-aggression Toward Inanimate Objects," *J. Exp. Anal. Behav.*, 1964, 7, 223–228. See also N. H. Azrin, R. R. Hutchinson, and R. McLaughlin, "The Opportunity for Aggression as an Operant Reinforcer During Aversive Stimulation," *J. Exp. Anal. Behav.*, 1965, 8, 171–180.

29 / 13 Fuegians   See Marston Bates, *Where Winter Never Comes* (New York: Charles Scribner's Sons, 1952), p. 102.

29 / 29 On feelings, see *COR*, n. 8.7.

29 / 34 John Stuart Mill, *Liberty* (1859), chap. 5.

31 / 5   positive reinforcement   See *SHB*, chaps. 5 and 6.

31 / 11 conditioned reinforcers   See *SHB*, p. 76.

32 / 7   Edmond and Jules de Goncourt, entry for July 29, 1860, *Journal: Mémoires de la vie littéraire* (Monaco, 1956).

32 / 15 schedules of reinforcement A brief account is in
             SHB, pp. 99–106. For an extensive experimental
             analysis, see *SR.*

33 / 23 self-control See *SHB*, chap. 15.

34 / 20 Bertrand de Jouvenel, *Sovereignty*, trans. J. F.
             Huntington (University of Chicago Press, 1957).

35 / 34 power to confer or withhold unlimited benefit
             Justice Roberts in *United States* v. *Butler*, 297
             U.S. 1, 56 Sup. Ct. 312 (1936).

36 / 1 motive or temptation not equivalent to coercion
             Justice Cardozo in *Steward Machine Co.* v. *Davis*,
             301 U.S. 548, 57 Sup. Ct. 883 (1937).

36 / 28 unrestricted freedom to reproduce or not to re-
             produce See a letter to *Science*, 1970, *167*, 1438.

37 / 27 Jean-Jacques Rousseau, *Émile ou de l' éducation*
             (1762).

42 / 32 Michel de Montaigne, *Essais*, III, ix (1580).

43 / 4 "knee-crooking knave" *Othello*, Act I, sc. I.

43 / 12 Rudyard Kipling, "The Vampire."

44 / 12 François, duc de La Rochefoucauld, *Maximes*
             (1665).

46 / 28 going two miles Matt. 5:41.

48 / 9 sounding trumpets Matt. 6:2.

50 / 8 creativity See B. F. Skinner, "Creating the Crea-
             tive Artist," in *On the Future of Art* (New York:
             The Viking Press, 1970). (To be reprinted in
             CR, 3rd edn.) Also see *SHB*, pp. 254–256.

53 / 17 J. F. C. Fuller, article on "Tactics," *Encyclopaedia
             Britannica*, 14th edn.

56 / 16 punishment See *SHB*, chap. 12.

58 / 24 Freudian dynamisms See *SHB*, pp. 376–378.

59 / 31 Biblical injunction Matt. 18:8.

62 / 11 T. H. Huxley, "On Descartes' *Discourse on
             Method*," in *Methods and Results* (New York:
             Macmillan, 1893), chap. 4.

62 / 16 See Joseph Wood Krutch, *The Measure of Man*
             (Indianapolis: Bobbs-Merrill, 1954), pp. 59–60.
             Mr. Krutch later reported that "few statments
             have ever struck me as more shocking. Huxley
             seemed to be saying that he would, if he could,
             be a termite rather than a man." ("Men, Apes,
             and Termites," *Saturday Review*, September 21,
             1963.)

66 / 16 Mill on goodness   See a review of James Fitz-
james Stephen, *Liberty, Equality, Fraternity,* in
Times Literary Supplement, October 3, 1968.

72 / 13 Raymond Bauer, *The New Man in Soviet Psychology* (Cambridge: Harvard University Press,
1952).

74 / 18 Joseph de Maistre   The passage was quoted in
the *New Statesman* for August–September 1957.

79 / 31 Socrates as midwife   Plato, *Meno.*

80 / 16 Freud and maieutics   Quoted from Walter A.
Kaufmann by David Shakow, "Ethics for a Scientific Age: Some Moral Aspects of Psychoanalysis," *The Psychoanalytic Review,* fall 1965, 52,
no. 3.

83 / 10 Alexis de Tocqueville, *Democracy in America,*
trans. Henry Reeve (Cambridge: Sever & Francis,
1863).

83 / 14 Ralph Barton Perry, *Pacific Spectator,* spring
1953.

87 / 13 prompts and hints   See *VB,* chap. 10.

89 / 13 operant discrimination   See *SHB,* chap. 7.

92 / 11 An editorial on abortion, *Time,* October 13, 1967.

98 / 25 positive reinforcers   See note for p. 31.

99 / 9 For the significance of reinforcers in the evolution
of the species, see *COR,* chap. 3.

99 / 23 "respondent" conditioning   See *SHB,* chap. 4.

100 / 19 On learning responses to private stimuli, see *SHB,*
chap. 17.

104 / 36 Eric Robertson Dodds, *The Greeks and the Irrational* (Berkeley: University of California Press,
1951).

106 / 29 "should" and "ought"   See *SHB,* p. 429.

108 / 18 Karl R. Popper, *The Open Society and Its Enemies*
(London: Routledge & Kegan Paul, 1947), p. 53.

110 / 5 For an extensive discussion of such agencies as
government, religion, economics, education, and
psychotherapy, see *SHB,* sec. 5.

112 / 27 Abraham H. Maslow, *Religions, Values, and
Peak-Experiences* (Columbus: Ohio State University Press, 1964).

118 / 2 Dante, *The Inferno,* canto 3.

118 / 18 Jean-Jacques Rousseau, *Dialogues* (1789).

121 / 9 the essential core of culture   Alfred L. Krober
and Clyde Kluckhohn, "Culture: A Critical Review
of Conceptions and Definitions," published in the
*Harvard University Peabody Museum of American
Archaeology and Ethnology Papers*, vol. 47,
no. 1 (Cambridge, 1952). (Paperback edn. 1963.)

124 / 14 the geography of Rome   See, for example, F. R.
Cowell, *Cicero and the Roman Republic* (London:
Pitman & Sons, 1948).

126 / 21 Social Darwinism   See Richard Hofstadter, *Social Darwinism in America Thought* (New York:
George Braziller, 1944).

132 / 23 Leslie A. White, *The Evolution of Culture* (New
York: McGraw-Hill Book Co., 1959).

135 / 10 language growing like an embryo   See Roger
Brown and Ursula Bellugi, "Three Processes in
the Child's Acquisition of Syntax," *Harvard Educational Review*, 1964, *34*, no. 2, 133–151.

135 / 13 the language of the feral child   Eric H. Lenneberg, in *Biological Foundations of Language*
(New York: John Wiley & Sons, Inc., 1967),
takes the contrary position of most psycholinguists
that some inner faculty fails to undergo "normal
development" (p. 142).

140 / 22 changing feelings   Feelings may seem to be
changed when we cheer a person up with a drink
or two or when he himself "reduces the aversive
features of his internal world" by drinking or by
smoking marijuana. But what is changed is not
the feeling but the bodily condition felt. The
designer of a culture changes the feelings which
accompany behavior in its relation to the environment, and he does so by changing the environment.

140 / 36 observing contingencies of reinforcement   See
COR, pp. 8–10.

143 / 5 contingency management   For a convenient collection of reports, see Roger Ulrich, Thomas
Stachnik, and John Mabry, eds., *Control of Human
Behavior*, vols. 1 and 2 (Glenview, Ill.: Scott,
Foresman & Co., 1966 and 1970).

146 / 6 utopias as experimental cultures   See *COR*, chap.
2.

146 / 17 behavioral utopias   Aldous Huxley's *Brave New
World* (1932) is no doubt the best known. It was
a satire, but Huxley recanted and tried his hand
at a serious version in *Island* (1962). The dominant psychology of the twentieth century, psychoanalysis, spawned no utopias. The author's
Walden Two describes a community designed
essentially on the principles which appear in the
present book.

150 / 12 Walter Lippmann, *The New York Times*, September 14, 1969.

153 / 32 Joseph Wood Krutch, *The Measure of Man* (Indi-
anapolis: Bobbs-Merrill, 1954).

155 / 25 "I wouldn't like it"   According to Mr. Krutch,
Bertrand Russell answered the complaint in this
way: "I do not disagree with Mr. Krutch as to
what I like and dislike. But we must not judge
the society of the future by considering whether
or not we should like to live in it; the question is
whether those who have grown up in it will be
happier than those who have grown up in our
society or those of the past." Joseph Wood Krutch,
"Danger: Utopia Ahead," *Saturday Review*, August 20, 1966. Whether people like a way of life
has to do with the problem of disaffection but
does not point to an ultimate value according to
which a way of life is to be judged.

157 / 9   Feodor Dostoevsky, *Notes from Underground*
(1864).

157 / 28 Arthur Koestler, *The Ghost in the Machine* (London: Hutchinson, 1967). See also "The Dark
Ages of Psychology," *The Listener*, May 14, 1964.

157 / 34 Peter Gay, *The New Yorker*, May 18, 1968.

159 / 3   *Times Literary Supplement* (London), July 11,
1968.

162 / 28 Ramakrishna   See Christopher Isherwood, *Ramakrishna and His Disciples* (London: Methuen,
1965).

165 / 10 According to Michael Holroyd, in *Lytton Strachey:
The Unknown Years* (London: William Heine-
man, 1967), G. E. Moore's concept of moral
conduct may be summarized as the intelligent
prediction of practical consequences. The im-

portant thing, however, is not to predict the consequences but to bring them to bear on the behavior of the individual.

166 / 19   the "pure" scientist   See P. W. Bridgman, "The Struggle for Intellectual Integrity," *Harper's Magazine*, December 1933.

167 / 3   "inborn need"   George Gaylord Simpson, *The Meaning of Evolution* (New Haven: Yale University Press, 1960).

167 / 24   See P. B. Medawar, *The Art of the Soluble* (London: Methuen & Co., Ltd., 1967), p. 51. According to Medawar, "Spencer's thought took on a darker complexion in later years for essentially thermodynamic reasons." He recognized the possibility of a "secular decay of order and dissipation of energy." A non-functional terminus is suggested in the maximizing of entropy. Spencer believed that evolution "came to an end when a certain state of equilibrium was reached."

167 / 27   Alfred Lord Tennyson, *In Memoriam* (1850).

168 / 32   superstition   See *SHB*, pp. 84–87.

169 / 27   leisure   See *COR*, pp. 67–71.

173 / 26   John Milton, *Paradise Lost*, bk. 1.

175 / 11   Crane Brinton, *Anatomy of a Revolution* (New York: W. W. Norton & Co., Inc., 1938), p. 195.

175 / 14   G. M. Trevelyan, *English Social History* (London: Longmans, Green and Co., 1942).

175 / 18   Gilbert Seldes, *The Stammering Century* (New York: Day, 1928).

179 / 1   learning to see and perceive   See *COR*, chap. 8.

180 / 19   rules and scientific knowledge   See *COR*, pp. 123–125 and chap. 6.

180 / 30   Vicol George Steiner, quoting Isaiah Berlin, *The New Yorker*, May 9, 1970, pp. 157–158.

181 / 13   consciousness and awareness   See *SHB*, chap. 17.

184 / 16   mental processes of generalizing, abstracting, and so on   See *COR*, pp. 274 ff., and *TT*, p. 120.

185 / 7   problem solving   See *SHB*, pp. 246–254 and *COR*, chap. 6.

186 / 13   On the interpretation of "physiological correlates," see *Brain and Conscious Experience* (New York: Springer-Verlag, 1966), which, according to a reviewer of the book ("Science and Inner Ex-

perience," by Josephine Semmes, *Science*, 1966, *154*, 754–756), reported a conference held "to consider the material basis of mental activity."

187 / 7   paleolithic bull   Attributed to Professor René Dubos by John A. Osmundsen, *The New York Times*, December 30, 1964.

187 / 26   internal copies of the environment   See *COR*, pp. 247 ff.

187 / 36   Wilson Follett, *Modern American Usage* (New York: Hill & Wang, 1966).

188 / 20   sin and sinful   See Homer Smith, *Man and His Gods* (Boston: Little, Brown, 1952), p. 236.

189 / 4   "something about Negroes themselves"   See *Science News*, December 20, 1969.

189 / 32   the self   See *SHB*, chap. 18.

190 / 30   Joseph Wood Krutch, "Epitaph for an Age," *New York Times Magazine*, June 30, 1967.

190 / 36   The quotation is from a review of Floyd W. Matson's *The Broken Image: Man, Science, and Society* (New York: George Braziller, 1964) in *Science*, 1964, *144*, 829–830.

191 / 3   Abraham H. Maslow, *Religions, Values, and Peak-Experiences* (Columbus: Ohio State University Press, 1964).

191 / 4   C. S. Lewis, *The Abolition of Man* (New York: Macmillan, 1957).

193 / 25   external source of power   J. P. Scott, "Evolution and the Individual," Memorandum prepared for Conference C, American Academy of Arts and Sciences Conferences on Evolutionary Theory and Human Progress (November 28, 1960).

198 / 15   Because of differences in the modes of transmission, a "generation" means very different things in biological and cultural evolution. With respect to cultural evolution it is little more than a measure of time. Changes in a culture ("mutations") may occur and be passed on many times in a single generation.

199 / 16   Étienne Cabet, *Voyage en Icarie* (Paris, 1848).

199 / 22   species   See Ernst Mayr, "Agassiz, Darwin and Evolution," *Harvard Library Bulletin*, 1959, *13*, no. 2.

202 / 15 Ernest Jones, *The Life and Work of Sigmund Freud* (New York: Basic Books, 1955).

203 / 9 historian H. Stuart Hughes, *Consciousness and Society* (New York: Alfred A. Knopf, 1958).

203 / 28 Keats on Newton Reported by Oscar Wilde in a letter to Emma Speed, March 21, 1882. Rupert Hart-Davis, ed., *The Letters of Oscar Wilde* (London, 1962).

Acknowledgments

Preparation of this book was supported by the National Institutes of Mental Health, Grant number K6-MH-21, 775—01.

Earlier discussions of some points will be found in "Freedom and the Control of Men," *The American Scholar* (winter 1955–56); "The Control of Human Behavior," *Transactions of the New York Academy of Sciences* (May 1955); "Some Issues concerning the Control of Human Behavior" (with Carl R. Rogers), *Science*, 1956, *124*, 1057–1066; "The Design of Cultures," *Daedalus* (1961 summer issue); and Section VI of *Science and Human Behavior*. The Mead-Swing Lectures given at Oberlin College in October 1959 were on the same theme.

For editorial and other help in the preparation of the manuscript I am much indebted to Carole L. Smith, and for a critical reading to George C. Homans.